LIES That Limit

Uncover the Truth of Who You Really Are

Teressa Moore Griffin

Praise for LIES That Limit:
Uncover the Truth of Who You Really Are

❧❧

"Once you read *LIES That Limit* and Teressa enters into your life, you will begin to shake loose long-held assumptions that can deform the way you think, feel and behave. I have seen how her presence instantly helps people to connect with their deeper selves, the self that knows the truth of who we really are and how to express our unique purpose. Why accept limits that don't exist?"

Bonnie St. John, author of *Live Your Joy*,
Olympic ski medalist and leadership consultant

"Teressa Moore Griffin takes you on exciting voyage of self-discovery. At every step of the way, you are confronted with the choice to either cling desperately to the LIES that limit self-realization or let them go. Every chapter is rich with profound insights and provocative challenges."

Barry Oshry, Director, Power + Systems, Inc.,
Author of Seeing Systems: Unlocking the Mysteries of Organizational Life

"Teressa's new book, *LIES That Limit*, provides us all with a roadmap that allows us to overcome the ceilings we build over our own heads. This is a must-read for every student, professional and executive that ever doubted themselves. Going forward *LIES That Limit* will be the bible for all budding entrepreneurs."

Larry Morris, former bond trader

"*LIES That Limit* opens the door to understanding one's true self and purpose in life. In a world saturated with messages that attempt to dictate who you should be, *LIES That Limit* helps you to get in touch with who you are. This book is truly a gift to be read by the whole family."

Michelle Drayton, President and Publisher, <u>Today's Child Magazine</u>

"Terrific! Teressa Moore Griffin gives the reader a richly rewarding book you want to read and reread. Her framework for growth provides new positive ways for viewing yourself in business and in life."

Barbara Pachter, speaker and author of *Greet! Eat! Tweet!* and *When The Little Things Count...And They Always Count*

"A true professional in the field of human understanding forces us to look in the mirror and make sure that we are telling ourselves the truth. This is an examination of what few dare face—the untruths that can serve as barriers to moving forward and dealing with life with a focused mind, and a real chance to finally clear the playing fields of our lives of the obstructions that block our chances for genuine happiness."

Larry Kane, TV personality and host of CN8's "Voice of Reason"

"Congratulations to author Teressa Moore Griffin for providing a poignant illustration on how we can truly connect our spirituality with our personal missions. Success comes to those who have profound understanding of the various ways in which to contribute positively—sustaining a just society."

Sylvia Watts McKinney, Executive Director,
Network for Teaching Entrepreneurship, Philadelphia Program

"Extreme gratitude and praise to Teressa Moore Griffin for sharing such a precious gem with the world. *LIES That Limit* is a deeply insightful and inspirational book packed full of practical tips for discovering, analyzing and overcoming the complex maze of emotional and psychological constraints— self-inflicted and imposed on us by others, our environment or circumstances — that prevent us from experiencing deep fulfillment, joy and abundance in all aspects of everyday life."

Rondo Moses, Managing Partner, Stratex Management Consulting

"This is a new path to inspired living, a way out of ruts you may not have known you were in!"

Tom Finn, author of *Are You Clueless? A Guide for Multicultural Leaders,*
www.areyouclueless.com

Dedication

To my mother and father – Cora Ellen Moore and Samuel Lee Moore – who provided me with the comforts and challenges needed for my growth.

To my Granny – Anna Lee Keels Moore – my extraordinary grandmother, nurturer, and caretaker.

To my brother – Lee Vern Moore – my playmate, constant ally, and objective voice of reason.

To my husband – William Griffin – my confidant, thought-partner, and supporter.

Table of Contents

Acknowledgements

I am grateful for the constant inspiration of Spirit, the Source of all the good I birth. The ideas and urges I receive — subtle and strong — lead to clear thinking and the courage to take right action. This book is one such inspiration.

Heartfelt thanks to my dear husband, Bill, Mom, Lee, Bill Woodson, Rondo Moses, Catharine Newberry, Edwina White, Mary Lou Michael, Jeanie Marshall, and many more who have listened to me talk as this book, and I, matured over the past fifteen years.

To the group who, in February 2004, allowed me to read raw, ragged notes to you over the course of two days, your expressed excitement about the possibility that my not yet fully formed ideas might turn in to a book motivated me. It meant a lot to go public with you, first. So, Debbie Cease, Tom Finn, Ferne Kuhn, Judith Leibowitz, Anne Litwin, Mary Lou Michael, Michelle Moomaugh, Elaine Robnett Moore, Peter Norlin, and Bill Woodson, thank you. You helped me take an important step in confronting my resistance to writing and my fear of "going public" with my message.

Sam Horn, you are an exceptional teacher and coach. Thanks for your many contributions to my development as a writer.

John and Shannon Tullius, I am fortunate to have found you and your Hawaii Writer's Retreat and Conference. I learned much from the excellent team of teachers you assemble, year after year. My Retreat experiences, first with Sam Horn, then later with Dan Millman, led to dramatic improvements in my writing. Know that I am grateful. And, who can argue with Hawaii as a venue for learning? Loved it!

Tom Finn, Kim Penn Gaskin, Rondo Moses, Linette (Sissy) Odd, Catharine Newberry, Kyle Ruffin, Pam Thomas, Lee and Lavinnie Moore — what a valuable service you provided as readers of the first draft of *LIES That Limit: Uncover the Truth of Who You Really Are*. Through questions and comments, each of you offered something special that led to a dramatic improvement in the manuscript. Your feedback was indeed a gift.

Tom Finn, Barbara Pachter, and Bonnie St. John, thanks for being close-up role models of professionals who write books that help people strengthen their competency as professionals and human beings.

To my mastermind team: you bring a depth of expertise and business savvy to the table. *And,* your passion and support for my vision is inspiring. Kim, you've been with me since the early days of dreaming about writing a book and building a community of people who are committed to Self-awareness. Thanks for the real-world practicalities you bring to bear in every conversation. Kyle, you have introduced me, and pushed me, to use modern tools I never imagined enjoying – blogging, Facebook, Twitter, television interviews – and you've been a great promotions partner. Pam, the boundless resource and connector, excellent researcher, and operations leader, your ability to keep things moving and on track is needed and appreciated.

To you, my corporate and private clients, all you've shared blessed me. I'm grateful that you allowed me into your work world, and for many, into your private lives. You are my mirrors and teachers.

Mom, you still call at just the right moment and ask the right question. Remember the Thursday afternoon you called and asked, "How's the book coming?" It was a moment when I was in a state of overwhelm, wondering if I could do this. Writing a book is a huge project! I told you I was drowning in the details. You said, "Teressa, you've never picked up anything you didn't finish and do well. This will be no different. You can do it." Like all in-tune mothers, you intuited what your child was up against and needed. Your call and encouragement came at just the right moment.

Lee, I appreciate your constant interest in me, and the book. Thanks for reading early drafts and providing feedback in a way that boosted my confidence. I am so glad you are my brother. You're the best!

Bill, you have heard it all, again and again. You've held me as I gnawed on and recoiled at the thought of writing a book, obsessed over the question of my ability to do it well, lost perspective and regained it, and finally emboldened myself and said, "Yes, I can, and I will." Thanks for cheering me on, standing strong, and being at my back. You supported me fully, quietly, providing what I needed in the moment – food, a listening ear, a clarifier, a reader, help with the daily details of living. Thank you for picking up the slack, for celebrating each milestone, and for loving me enough to give me the space to birth this baby. It means a lot to have a partner who never complains when I disappear to meditate, write, rewrite, and write again.

Wes Moore, to you and your remarkable mother, Joy, I'm so fortunate to have met you. I admire your work, *The Other Wes Moore,* and I appreciate your support and guidance. Howard and Pam, thanks for the introduction that lovely Christmas eve, some years ago.

Kristin Coffey, editor extraordinaire, you were amazingly helpful. Joy, thank you for connecting us. Every conversation with you, Kristin, resulted in important improvements to *LIES That Limit: Uncover the Truth of Who You Really Are*. Happily, I'm the beneficiary of your professional excellence. Your calm, nonjudgmental demeanor makes you a pleasure to work with.

If you helped me in any way, and you were not named, please know that the oversight is unintended. I am thankful to you for your contribution.

With boundless gratitude,
Teressa

Foreword by Wes Moore

For years, I believed that just getting by was good enough. My view of the world was clouded by a constant mist of uncertainty, anger, and self-doubt, all masking the purpose and promise of the boy I really wanted to be. My grades were mediocre, my behavior sporadic, and my youthful journey to manhood was peppered with examples of negative self-fulfilling prophecies that stood in the way of true happiness and success.

But as I got older and my journey to manhood continued its serpentine route, I began to realize that my life might have greater meaning if I could shed the negative feelings and influences that were limiting my growth. Had Teressa Moore Griffin's book *LIES That Limit* been available to me and the mentors who touched my life, I might have come to the realization of my life's purpose much earlier.

LIES That Limit: Uncover the Truth of Who You Really Are will help readers understand the practical part of living their purpose by reinforcing the truth that each of us was intentionally created by a loving God to do something specific with our lives. It identifies a host of LIES — Labels, Illusions, Excuses, and Stories — that creep into too many of our lives, and provides tools to help us confront these untruths that keep us locked in roles that are unsatisfying and in some cases destructive. Utilizing a narrative and workbook-type approach, *LIES That Limit* also provides a unique road map that shows us what to do next, so we don't get stuck or paralyzed by indecision.

LIES that Limit shares stories of real people Ms. Moore Griffin has worked with over the years as an executive coach, whose tales may mirror our own lives and can help us ask questions that we didn't know we needed to ask. As her clients found, sometimes we need permission to get to know who we really are and what we're here to contribute to the world. This book provides that permission and encourages us to follow our dreams back to the happiness we knew as children, but have lost sight of as adults.

Ms. Moore Griffin shows us the pitfalls of the LIES we live every day, and simultaneously, teaches us to use our talents, gifts, and abilities to the fullest — which is the core of living a purposeful and fulfilling life.

This is an interactive book to be read carefully and mindfully. Engage in the journaling and self-probing you're invited to do. See what more you uncover of your deeper self. Notice how much more self-aware, clear-thinking, and confident you become — all with the benefit of helping you, as it did me, become even more positive and productive in every aspect of your life.

Wes Moore, bestselling author, *The Other Wes Moore: One Name, Two Fates*
www.theotherwesmoore.com

Introduction

From the earliest time I can remember, I felt there was something more to life – something more than I knew or had experienced. I was certain there was something more grand, amazing, and glorious out there for me. I felt called, compelled to find it.

Ceaselessly, I searched, looking in all the places I was told to look — in achievement and creature comforts, in relationships, in work and overwork, in religion. Nowhere did I find the answer to my longing. I wanted sustained satisfaction and deep and abiding peace. I wanted to experience joy and love – positive, affirmative feelings that would endure. I found many good and enjoyable things. But, at no time did the feeling of "grand, amazing, and glorious" last very long.

Yet, the call persisted, and so did my searching. My deep need to find "something more" never quit. No matter how much I tried to push it down, silence it, ignore it, wish it away, or placate it, it would not take "No!" for an answer. It demanded my attention and inspired my quest to know more.

I wanted answers to the mysteries of life. I wanted to know:

- Who am I? It certainly seemed like there was more to me than just a brain, body, and personality. But, what is it?
- What am I doing here, anyway? Do I have a purpose? If so, what is it? What am I here to do?
- God, what do You want me to do? What do You want me to think? How do You want me to feel? How do You want me to live?
- Am I doing the right thing with my life? Am I on the right path?

I wanted answers, and I wanted them from God. I wanted to be in communication with The Divine.

Interestingly enough, I received answers to my questions. You'll discover some of what I learned in this book. Contrary to the logic and wisdom I had heard all my life, the content of the messages stopped me in my tracks. I began to question more of what I had been taught to believe.

The gift I received was greater insight into the fallacy of the way I think, feel, and behave. More important, I began to see the faults and limits associated with many revered social traditions.

LIES That Limit is about the Labels, Illusions, Excuses, and Stories (LIES) that we allow to comprise the majority of what we believe to be true about ourselves, others, and the world. In this book I'll share what I've learned through personal experiences and from the thousands of people, around the world, I've been privileged to work with during my career as a human resources professional and manager in the retail, financial, and pharmaceutical industries, and in my more than twenty-three years as an international organization development consultant and executive coach.

This is an empirical and practical book, not an academic, theoretical work. And, this simple idea – LIES limit – has changed the way I see my Self, everyone, and everything around me. It has also influenced the way I work with my clients, most of whom are senior executives in Fortune 1000 companies.

The concept of *LIES That Limit* has pushed me to my growing edge – the place where I left aspects of myself and must reclaim in order to feel my wholeness. I hope it will do the same for you because, in small and large ways, LIES have limited your conception and knowledge of who you really are. Accordingly, your understanding of your potential and purpose pales in comparison to what is actually true and possible.

LIES are taught and perpetuated through the *labels* we are given and the ways we label others; *illusions* we hold about reality; *excuses* we make for ourselves and others who face similar conditions; and the *stories* we tell with emotion, over and over again. The more we hear them, the more LIES sound like immutable facts.

LIES That LIMIT is a slim book because TRUTH requires few words; it presents itself simply, clearly, and honestly. The work comes as you live TRUTH and apply it to every situation and circumstance in your life.

The first in my series of books, *LIES That LIMIT* helps you uncover the Truth of who you really are. When you get in touch with the deeper reality of the amazing, creative, limitless being you are, you'll look at life — yours in particular — differently. Viewing life through these lenses, your day-to-day existence will improve. The way you relate to yourself and the world around you will be transformed. You'll find more meaning and purpose, more clarity and peace, more love and joy. You'll feel stronger and whole.

The goal of this book is to let go of the LIES that stop you from being who you were born to be. You will identify the ways you hide your true Self so you can live a better, saner life — a life that ultimately leads to greater effectiveness, peace of mind, and more love, courage, satisfaction, and success.

LIES that LIMIT provides practical, easy-to-use tools that will help you uncover more ways to create the life you want. Find yourself in the stories, faithfully apply the ideas, and watch what happens. Notice how you begin to feel less and less like a victim of circumstance. Notice how more and more you feel accountable, clear, confident, in charge, and wise. When you're empowered to take effective action, the voice of fear and resistance subsides. In its place, the voice of wisdom claims prominence.

You're much more grand than you know. You are Spirit — the creative, divine energy that animates your body, the consciousness that witnesses all you do — and you have a Purpose. *You are a Spirit of Purpose.*

Your decision to read this book means you're interested in unmasking your deeper, wiser nature. You've decided to understand the LIES — the Labels, Illusions, Excuses, and Stories — you live, and the ways you make them your reality. You're looking within to get to know your true Self, instead of living stories others have created for you.

The journey you take in life is not your Spirit's or Soul's journey; it's the journey of your personality, your limited, little, ego-based, scared self. On that journey, all too often and unnecessarily, you suffer. You feel you've wandered far away from your core and center. You're in a land distant from the safety and sanctity of home. You fear you've strayed from truth, love, and wholeness. But, it's your personality that travels into the wilderness, seemingly alone. Your Spirit walks with you, protects you, and waits for you to awaken and recognize who you really are. Spirit whispers gently, "Let go of the LIES that limit you."

Know this: no matter how far away you wander, nothing can keep TRUTH from being what it is. Are you ready to journey home and reconnect with your Spirit of Purpose and experience the depth of satisfaction that is rightfully yours?

If you've ever said to yourself, "There must be more to life than *this*," then your deeper Self is calling to you. The call is for a release from the ways you imprison your Self. Answer the call. Get to know the real you – the more alive and powerful, more self-responsible and accountable you – that is *not* defined by Labels, Illusions, Excuses, and Stories.

How to Read and Work With LIES That Limit

❦

LIES That Limit requires your active engagement because it encourages in-depth self-exploration. If you would like suggestions for getting the most from this book, here are a few tips.

First, read the book and allow the ideas it contains to wash over you. You may even want to highlight or underline key points that interest you and perspectives that speak to you and feel relevant to your life. Then, reread the book and write out your responses to the questions in the sections labeled **Journal Your Truth**. The journal questions are located at the end of each chapter.

After you've reread the book and written out your responses to the **Journal Your Truth** questions, read through your entries and look for patterns in your comments. See what a review of your entries teaches you about the ways you hold on to beliefs and behaviors that no longer serve you. Notice where you're sidetracked and where you hold yourself back. Become more self-observant and self-aware — tune in to how you limit your capacity to self-actualize; to be the full and amazing being you are — a Spirit with a Purpose.

Write down the thoughts, feelings, memories, ideas, images, and intuitions that come. They provide insight into the ways you're still guided by negative messages and experiences from your past; the undue present-day influences of unfounded and outdated social conventions; and most important, enlightenment about who you really are and the Purpose you were born to fulfill.

Pay attention to synchronistic events — things that seem to be an interesting coincidence. You may read something about LIES and later that day hear a news story or a conversation, or witness an interaction, that is a demonstration of exactly what you were reading or thinking about. You may react to someone, triggered by one of the LIES described in the book or one that exists in your life. Take these moments seriously. They are showing you something important about you and can become a *Pivot Point* in your life — a time when you choose to turn from one way of reacting to another. You'll read more about *Pivot Points* in later chapters.

Look for the tools and techniques that may be useful to you as you work to know more about the deeper you. While there is a section of the book devoted to tools and techniques, you'll find proven processes and ideas throughout.

LIES That Limit is intended to be a partner in your evolution — your process of self-awareness and personal growth. It's a book you read and read, highlight and reread key passages, because the work of ridding your life of LIES is ongoing. When you do the work described herein, you'll clear away the debris that clutters your mind and baggage that weighs heavy on your heart — all of which rob you of the exercise of free will and the right to self-rule.

Dig deep and recover your truth — your Spirit and sense of Purpose. The being you were born to be awaits your return. Turn the page and take an important step on your journey of self-inquiry, self-discovery, and enhanced self-awareness.

Chapter One

Parts of You and Me

☙❧

Who We Are

There are multiple dimensions to our being – different parts or aspects of our personality and identity. These parts – some well known to us, some only vaguely recognizable, and others totally unfamiliar – create the composite that makes us who we are. Everyone has his or her own unique composition of parts.

Think of the aspects you are well acquainted with as parts of you that live out in the open, visible and accepted as the you you know. Like an old friend, these parts are acknowledged and feel comfortable. Vaguely familiar and unfamiliar aspects live in the dark shadows and recesses and rarely see the light of day.

It's good to be familiar with your full range of aspects – the parts with which you have a close relationship, a distant relationship, and no relationship. Otherwise, you miss your depth and diversity, and find yourself living with strangers within – strangers who behave in certain ways or react to particular circumstances and that leave you wondering why you did *that* or how *that* happened.

Strangers within – these unfamiliar dimensions of your being – are more influential than you know. Because they wield such power, it's good to get to know them, befriend them, and develop a peaceful relationship. These shadow figures can work in your favor and support you or they can be your saboteurs. You need to know who lives within. It's wise to know all parts of you – the parts that drive toward you being your best and living your dreams, and the parts that push against your conscious wishes and derail you. Unmasking and surfacing all parts of you and inviting them out into the light of day is a big part of what *LIES That Limit* is designed to help you do.

There are many ways to become better acquainted with the many parts of your persona. Self-analysis based on keen observation is a primary and important route to deepening self-awareness. Reading self-help books, participating in personal growth experiences, or working with a trained therapist are other viable ways of becoming more familiar with all parts of your character and behavioral patterns. Dreams — both daydreams and nighttime dreams — are another tool that can provide amazing perspective into our many selves.

Discovering Parts of Me

Dreams have always played a significant role in my life. They offer valuable information and perspective. The story you are about to read was a nighttime dream I had in 1996, after my first month-long trip to south India. I've had many wonderful extended trips to India since then, but, during my first visit, I had a strong and disconcerting emotional reaction to what I experienced.

All of my senses were assaulted. I experienced unending noise, day and night; an array of odors — sometimes the lovely fragrance of sandalwood or jasmine and at other times the stench of raw sewage and everything in between; there were people everywhere. Throngs of people made for big crowds; I felt overwhelmed and squeezed out by the lack of physical and personal space. I was stared at and pointed to; often people would come closer to look at me. Poverty, evident everywhere, was sometimes juxtaposed against the opulent beauty of palaces and grand homes or wonderfully colorful saris woven with golden threads worn by women whose wealth was evident. Class and caste were clear and conspicuous.

I took my energy and tucked myself away into a tiny ball at the base of my skull, behind my brain. I stayed there until I returned home. I went numb. It was the best I could do. I had to survive and disappearing from undesirable circumstances was the path I chose.

After my return, late one evening a friend called to ask about my trip. I laid into my long list of complaints. "It was miserably hot with inadequate air conditioning; it rained and I had to wade in knee-deep water with who knows what in it; people stared and pointed at me everywhere I went; it was noisy, too crowded, dirty, and smelled terrible; there was poverty everywhere – hoards of poor people, from tiny children to adults, many of whom were physically deformed or disabled, all begging for crumbs."

On and on I went. My friend listened patiently. Then, she said, "I wonder what you're to learn from this?" You can imagine my reaction.

"Learn from this? You must be kidding. I've learned more on a trip to the grocery store." With that, we said good night. Shortly after the call, I went to bed and had an amazing, illuminating dream that introduced me to different parts of my persona. Some aspects were familiar friends or at least acquaintances, and other parts were total strangers. No wonder I had such a strong reaction to my initial experience of India! I had a lot to learn from this experience, if only my arrogance and judgmentalness would subside enough to allow truth and insight to shine forth. Sleep was the state that made a deep look into my being possible. My conscious mind was not there judging, interfering, and blocking access to expanded self-perception.

The dream I had that night fascinated me and seemed prophetic. It provided a window into known and unexplored aspects of my being. I wrote it down and studied it. The more I interacted with it, the more important and instructive it felt. Retelling the dream begins with the next paragraph and continues through to my method of interpreting the meaning of the dream and the reality of the parts of me revealed by the dream.

It was my last night in India. I returned to my hotel room, packed and prepared for the trip home. Upon entering my room, I saw two beautiful little girls, sisters, about four and five. Wearing identical dresses with black and white plaid taffeta bottoms and a black velvet bodice, black patent Mary Jane shoes, with white tights, their clothing and manner made their social station clear. They were children from an upper-class, privileged family.

The girls were beautiful, sweet, open, loving, warm, friendly, and trusting even of me, a stranger. Without hesitation, they invited me to join them in their game. As we played, they captured my heart, the youngest one in particular. She was amazingly loving and lovable. Though loving, the older of the two had already learned to be aloof. Her interaction was tinged with suspicion. Mistrust was in her watchful eyes and the stiffening of her body. She had already learned to withhold her Self and to interact cautiously. She was no longer as relaxed and free as her younger sister.

Time passed and the girls talked and played. Often, the little one would stop playing and come over and stand in front of me, her hands on my knees. Through the energy of her presence, she made it known she wanted me to look into her eyes and touch her face. Each time she made the request, I complied. In those moments, I said to myself, "This child's only purpose is to give and receive love." Moved by the depth and intensity of our connection my heart opened. I was in awe of the depth of our exchange.

Before long, their mother arrived. She was in her early thirties, very attractive, busy, and successful. Surprisingly, like me, she was an organization development consultant, from Harrisburg, Pennsylvania. As we talked more, I realized she was a friend of my dear friend, Kim Penn Gaskin. We laughed about how small the world is.

Later, the maternal grandmother of the two little girls appeared. Stunningly attractive, well educated, well traveled and sophisticated, she lived in Europe. She was calm, confident, self-possessed, and full of love and strength. I admired her instantly and enjoyed her company. She had amazing life stories and took pleasure in telling them. I loved listening and having a glimpse into the life of a woman who gave herself full freedom to be herself, to take up space, to be seen in all her beauty, softness, and power. To me, this woman was a marvel.

As I interacted with the girls and talked with their mother and grandmother, I became aware of how deeply sad and fearful I felt. My emotional and physical energy felt heavy, dense, and hopeless, even as I tried hard to be light-hearted and playful. I was keenly aware of my caste in contrast to theirs.

Born into a cultural group of former Untouchables, I was from a subservient caste. We were the "less-than" people, the social slaves. I wanted to escape the burden of my lot and find freedom. Trembling and afraid, I decided to shed my shackles. The older woman told me she would help me escape. I was delighted. And, there was just one problem: The Border Patrol.

The Border Patrol was fierce and unmerciful. I feared capture. I had all the visible markings of my caste. Everything from my skin color to the texture of my hair to my level of education to my speech pattern to the burdened and broken-down way I walked to the appearance of my teeth to the clothes I wore — it all gave away my identity. The Border Patrol was sure to spot me and stop me from leaving the country. I shared my fears with the wise and wonderful woman. Together we devised a clever plan for my safe passage across the border.

My companion for the journey to freedom was a young woman from a high Indian caste. She agreed to use the privilege and authority ascribed to those of her group to help me move through the checkpoint. Arriving at the border between the life I knew and the one I longed for, predictably, we came face to face with the guards.

As they questioned my travel companion, my guide and protector, I dared not make eye contact with them. Not wanting them to see the terror in my eyes, I looked away, peering out through the window and across the barren field that marked the land this side of the border. She did all the talking. I tried to appear unconcerned. Though The Border Patrol didn't truly believe her story, the guards chose not to tangle with her. Crossing over the border, we arrived safely on the other side. Finally, I was free.

Free?!?! I knew it; I could think the thought and say the word freedom, but I couldn't feel it. My body was still trembling and numb, frozen with fear. In my mind's eye, it seemed I should want to jump and shout and scream and celebrate. Excitement coursing throughout her body, my companion for the journey squeezed my left hand and saying "You're Free! You're Free!" Clearly, she was happy for me.

In that moment, at that time and in that place, I knew I was free, but fear blocked my ability to feel free. I was still afraid The Border Patrol would come, claim me, and take me back to that place of subservience, slavery, and bondage.

In truth, I had never been an Untouchable or a slave. I had the legal liberty to move about as I pleased. But, based on the way I was treated, I felt like a slave. On a psychological level, I and all others in the culture were in collusion to keep me in my "place."

To be free is to be physically, mentally, and emotionally emancipated — liberated from constraining, socially imposed definitions and cultural conditioning. To be free is to be released from the mind-numbing fear and controlling influence of The Border Patrol.

Freedom means moving beyond limited definitions of who I am and what is possible for me — definitions that limit awareness of my deeper Self. Such limits are

LIES that restrict options, movement, and progress; hold me back; and cause me to repeat or relive parts of a past that no longer serve me. Freedom means I am no longer prisoner to self-sabotage and self-oppression. Instead, freedom means I become the wise woman who is able to lead me safely beyond The Border Patrol, to a new place where I live without social constraints that hinder self-awareness and expression of my Spirit and Purpose.

That was my dream. When I awakened, I knew I had been given a gift that would give to me over and over again. I wrote down the dream, determined to distill every ounce of learning and insight I could extract. While I'm not a dream analyst for anyone else, I'm an extraordinary analyst for myself. I use a method of dream interpretation called Percept, a technique developed by John and Joyce Weir. I learned the technique from the Weirs and Alexandra Merrill. Percept Language encourages you to see all parts of a dream, animate and inanimate, or any situation to which you apply the technique, as parts of you. It can be incredibly illuminating.

I applied the technique to my dream. Some parts or players in the dream were recognized, active components of my life. Living in the light of my awareness, I was aware of these parts of me and identified with them easily. Other parts were outside of my awareness, living in the shadows. The dream, and this method of interpretation, brought these hidden dimensions to light.

At the time of this dream, I was most acquainted with the busy organization and leadership development consultant part of me. That was my primary identity, a role I lived daily and enjoyed. I was also aware of the five-year-old part of me – the longing to be loved and loving, but feeling too cautious and suspicious to give and receive love without reservation on my part. Well trained, she bought into the cultural norm of holding back and not giving *too* much for fear of being *too* open and *too* vulnerable. Both openness and vulnerability, she had been taught, were dangerous and naïve; she *could* get hurt.

Familiarity with the oppressed part of me, the Untouchable, slave girl in me, had been growing. Appearing to be about nineteen years old, she wanted and tried to be happy, but the labels and stories she understood to be "reality" for people like her — slave girl, less than, under class, low caste — were all too burdensome and constricting to bear. Terrified or not, like Harriett Tubman, this part of me was willing to risk the threat of shame, ostracism, imprisonment, even death in order to be free to create my life as I wanted it to be. This part of me thought oppression was created by the place and conditions in which I found myself.

The image of *The Border Patrol* part of me was shocking. The presence of this menacing, uniformed, gun-toting, non-thinking, rule-following, fearless, Gestapo-like character got my attention. Though I had some awareness of ways in which I held myself back from doing what I desired, the fear of failure represented in my dream by *The Border Patrol* was the main culprit. The dream and this particular image provided a shake-up and wake-up call.

The Border Patrol wielded power — inspecting, questioning, scrutinizing, and meting out all manner of known and unknown punishment. Its oppressiveness was designed to control through fear and keep me in my place. The mere idea of this part of me ran contrary to every articulated message I'd ever received. Nowhere in any cultural training or formal education did anyone say that the most powerful oppressor was within me. The explicit messages I received never suggested that I was my primary oppressor; the finger of blame always pointed outward to *them* and *those people*. But here I was, being taught by a dream to see my role in maintaining the border between the life that burdened and saddened me, and the life I desperately wanted.

It was an illusion that the oppressor existed only out there in *them* or *those people*. It was an illusion, a false statement, no matter how frequently and convincingly stories were told and examples provided to prove the point. It was one of the LIES that sounded like truth and was treated as fact.

LIES are fine lines that mark the border between a life of blame, denial of self-responsibility, disempowerment, and a self-righteous sense of victimization and a life defined by the success and satisfaction that comes from being self-responsible and accountable — listening to my heart's desires and taking action, however risky, to live in alignment with my purpose and calling.

There I was, faced with the fact that the oppressor, *The Border Patrol*, was a part of me. It lived in *me* and was nurtured by *me*. I colluded with its menacing presence and reinforced its power each time I recoiled in fear instead of pushing the boundaries. The Labels, Illusions, Excuses, and Stories of *The Border Patrol* were designed to keep it, and you, in place. The story in the world is *others* do it to you, not that *you* oppress yourself.

Now, with new awareness, I was on the lookout for the part of me that polices me, protects the status quo, keeps me from fearlessly "coming out," and reinforces unnecessary rules and restrictions concerning acceptable choices and what's out of bounds for "people like me."

The younger of the two girls, the one who intentionally connected with me solely for the purpose of giving and receiving love, and the grandmother are also parts of me – core essence, these parts of me are loving, unencumbered by LIES and limitations. They are open, giving, able to receive, confident, calm, self-possessed, and clear about who they are and what they want.

My guide and travel companion, undaunted by *The Border Patrol,* is my Spirit. She is the ageless, nameless, courageous, ever-present part of me; a witness to all I think and do and feel. She looks out for me, takes care of me, paves the way, keeps me out of harm's way, is my courage when needed, steadies me, and helps me move beyond my self-imposed limits. She is with me on my never-ending journey that is the unfolding of my life and purpose.

Spirit

Everyone's Spirit is his or her ever-present companion and guide. If only we'd listen to our inner voice and allow it to lead us on the journey. If only we'd let Spirit do the talking and walking. If only! But, we don't.

Through conditioning we blind ourselves to the best of who we are. We become untrusting, too busy, too intellectual, too committed to rules and ideas that, in the end, don't serve our growth or expand awareness of our Spirit and Purpose. We collude with the internal *Border Patrol,* limiting our self-expression and access to what is best and right for us. We become too afraid to touch our core, our Spirit, our own divine nature.

Spirit is the only part of you that's always with you — it contains everything that matters and endures. Spirit is the keeper of unchanging universal truth. Spirit is where the search for everything ends. Once you connect with your core or Spirit, you've found everything worthy of your attention and devotion.

The Border Patrol

What's in the way of accessing your true nature? LIES. You allow LIES — the cultural story about what's true, real, and important — to come between you and your Spirit. LIES dull the connection to your core and your calling. LIES, enforced by *The Border Patrol*, make you afraid to let your Spirit rule your life, guide your actions and decisions, and keep you aligned with the truth of who you really are.

Convincingly, *The Border Patrol* will say, "If you start talking about this weird, woo-woo stuff, you'll lose everything you've worked so hard to achieve and acquire." *The Border Patrol* will persuade you to stay out of that foreign territory of Spirit and Purpose and keep your feet planted firmly on the ground. It will tell you to leave all that nonsense alone, and threaten you with, "If you don't, you'll become an outcast, ridiculed and humiliated for your beliefs — rejected by the people who love you."

Adopting the ways of the world, what you mistakenly call life takes center stage. Your connection with your core Self is lost. Soon, you forget you're the creative force in your life. You give up authorship. You lose faith in your ability to be sure of who you are, why you're here, and what's right for you. The controlling, self-sabotaging power of *The Border Patrol* takes the driver's seat in your mind.

The Border Patrol is expert at generating fear of losing love. In reality, no one could ever love you less than this internal agent of oppression. When speaking to you, *The Border Patrol's* words seem logical, make sense, and sound reasonable and protective. After all, you don't want to jeopardize your safety and security. But, what you don't understand is its cunning, loveless nature. Blindly, you yield to the authority of *The Border Patrol*, agreeing to live LIES in exchange for a false sense of security. Talk about selling your soul to the devil!

Journal Your Truth

Which parts of your personality are you most familiar with?

Which aspects have you glimpsed, but are less familiar with?

These are the strangers within.

What role do dreams play in your life — both daydreams and nighttime dreams?

What is the child, or children, within you like?
- Age or ages?
- Personality characteristics?
- Physical appearance, posture, and bearing?

Are you aware of the Wise One within?
- Age?
- Gender?
- Describe your Wise One's energy and way of being — its persona?
- Physical appearance, posture, bearing?

Are you aware of The Border Patrol that guards your mind?
- Describe it.
- What does it look like?
- What triggers it into action?
- What are its characteristic ways of keeping you contained within familiar territory?

Chapter Two

Born Knowing

✿

The Beginning and the Ending

At both ends of life, we have the greatest potential for clarity and we know the truth of who we are, what we want, and what's important. Why is that? It's because in that big middle space between the beginning (birth) and the ending (death) we lose close connection to our true essence.

Early on, the knowledge of our real Self — the self that is way more than our personality and habits — is clear to us. We know our particular brand of genius. In later years, if we're among the fortunate, we rediscover our truth — the reality of our individual uniqueness, purpose, and passion. Whenever it comes, such clarity is a gift.

But oh, those middle years — the time when the mind-training takes hold and *The Border Patrol* becomes an integrated, self-policing aspect of your mind — are the years when you give up a great deal of choice and control. Doing so is in your best interest, or so you're told.

Born to Be a Superstar

In the beginning, you're aligned with the miracle that you are. Knowing you're here to be creative and free, you naturally express your passion and gifts. Nothing blocks access to your authentic Self. Its presence awakens the joyful child, the patient inner guide, and the loving, radiant wise one within.

When my godchild was about five years old, I asked her, "Kamryn, what do you want to be when you grow up?"

Sensing the question's importance, Kamryn stopped playing with her brother. She stepped closer to the kitchen table where her mother and I sat, enjoying the energy of these happy children at play. Looking me straight in the eyes, she said, "Auntie Teressa, I don't know yet. I was born to be a superstar. I'm great at so many things."

"Tell me what you're good at," I asked, encouraging conversation and wanting a glimpse of all she was contemplating.

She put her hands on her tiny hips, tilted her head to the left and lifted her eyes toward the ceiling. Then, with her list clarified, she confidently told me, "I could be a doctor, an actress, a writer, a singer, a dancer, a mom, a cheerleading coach, an executive like my mom, a teacher, a hairdresser, a leader. I'm a really good leader. Or, I could be an athlete because I'm strong and fast."

With excitement in her voice and self-assured body language, she reminded me, "I have a lot of choices. I'm good at so many things."

She was right. She was and is good at so many things. Delighted to witness her unself-conscious pure confidence, her mother and I looked at each other and smiled, she was merely telling the truth. Fully aware of her brilliance and her destiny, without shame of bragging, Kamryn gave voice to the kind of abilities that, early on, you and I feel and know exists in each of us.

Children readily confess and demonstrate their extraordinary talent — the special gifts with which they're endowed. While specific words may not be available to them, they sense something that is theirs to be and do. They feel the call of their Purpose. They know the truth of who they are. Their thoughts, feelings, and behaviors are aligned with their Spirit and particular Purpose. Kamryn provides us with an example of how lucid children can be, particularly those whose light has not been dimmed by the strong shadow of negativity.

A child's passion and purpose show up in play. Their special spirit is evident. If they're not controlled and oppressed by those around them, the essence of who they are is accessible and freely expressed.

My brother Lee's life provides another example.

Lee's Prophesy: My Future Is in Garbage

Until I was eight years old and my brother was six, we lived in Greeleyville, South Carolina. In our small, rural town, during the 1950s and 1960s, garbage was burned. As trash accumulated, we threw it into a heap, at the far edge of the backyard, near the woods.

Tending the pile was Lee's favorite job. He was the self-designated authority on its neatness and size, what was to be composted, and what was set aside for burning.

On a day when the wind was blowing away from the house and shed, all sticks, leaves, bramble, anything dry, and obviously flammable would be picked up and thrown onto the mound. Water was poured, saturating the ground around the pile in an attempt to prevent the fire from spreading. The trash pile would be set ablaze, Lee and I would help with several buckets of water positioned at the ready to dampen errant sparks before they could do any damage. Once the fire consumed the rubbish, water was poured on the ashes, extinguishing the embers.

In May of 1963, Lee and I arrived home to find smoke curling from embers in the place where, that morning, our house stood. Homeless, that June our family moved to Bristol, Pennsylvania; a small town northeast of Philadelphia. There, the process for getting rid of trash was remarkably different.

Every Tuesday and Friday, men came along in a dark green truck and collected it from the curb just outside the front door. One man drove the truck and two others rode standing up, on the ledge of the truck's black back bumper. For safety, they held on to a handle built into the truck's frame. One man was positioned on the left side of the back bay of the truck and the other was situated on the right.

The driver motored slowly down the block. The two men on the back would jump down, grab the garbage cans filled with trash, and dump them into the opening in the back of the truck. One of the two collectors would then pull a lever, closing the bay. As the door came down, a motor inside made a loud growling and grinding noise. It smashed the trash, making space for garbage at the next house.

This process and these men fascinated Lee. He ran alongside the truck, or rode his bike, keeping pace with the driver, witnessing the work of the men who rode standing up on the truck's bumper.

With that as a backdrop, you can probably guess my little brother's answer to the question, "What do you want to be when you grow up?" You've got it. Proudly he would respond, "A garbage man!" His announcement came without shame. It was what he loved and wanted to do.

Lee is an example of how passion and purpose show up early in life, even if others don't understand or approve.

A child's interests may strike those around him as desirable and the grown-ups approve of the child's curiosity or fascination. At other times, what captivates a child's imagination may be dismissed, considered child's play, not a good way to make a living, or an improbable and impossible dream. Well-meaning adults may do their best to talk the child out of what he loves because they think it's not a wise choice, long term. But, the child is prophesying his future. Passion and purpose are persistent. They demand satisfaction. That's one of many things my brother has taught me.

Over the course of his now more than thirty-year career, Lee tried his hand at a number of positions and in various industries. From hardware sales to risk management and industrial safety in the oil industry, his route ultimately led him back to his passion — garbage men and their trucks. Through a set of events that seemed serendipitous, he landed in the place of his early fascination.

Today, my brother runs the waste management operation for a city in Oklahoma. He's in charge of the men and the trucks that pick up the trash. My sister-in-law, Lavinnie, tells the story of the day she met Lee. She asked him what he did for a living. His reply: "I'm a garbage man." He's right. Garbage, garbage men, and their trucks have held his fascination ever since he was a little boy. His childhood fascination was a prophesy about his future. Who knew?

It's interesting to think about. Early on, we know what we love, even if those around us don't see it as worthy of our talent, or not the kind of work or career path that will produce reasonable earning opportunities or status commensurate with their expectations for us. But we love what we love. And, in that love there is evidence of our calling for what we are here to do.

Acting Out Their Dreams

Kamryn and Lee, like most children, share details concerning what excites them and stirs their imagination. Acting out their gifts in play, we can visualize their talents and the kind of people they will become.

Observing their behaviors, even a stranger can envision who they will become. I had such an experience one warm, beautiful December afternoon as I watched three children at play.

They were enjoying the afternoon sand and surf on St. John's Great Cruz Bay. The boy was about seven or eight, and as for the two little girls, one was about six and the other around four. Evidence suggested that the six-year-old would someday be the boss of something and lots of people. Over the course of several hours of serious play, she demonstrated as much.

She had her workers, the boy and the younger girl, building sand castles. She gave them orders. "Build it three stories tall." She gave them feedback. "You're not working fast enough. Work faster." She coached them. "Make it neater, like this," showing the other two the proper technique.

Occasionally, she made a call on her pretend mobile phone, telling the imaginary listener something important.

Turning back to her workers, she encouraged them. "That's better. We have to work fast and get this job done. We have to get paid. Keep working. We don't have much time to finish."

That young lady was a credible leader. She exerted influence and kept her workers moving and focused on the task at hand. Twenty or thirty years from that day, she's bound to be the boss. She is a natural; effective at leading those younger and older, comfortable with power, and confident in her right to exercise it.

Children communicate their interests through their choice of roles when at play, the images they draw and the content of their conversation. They unwittingly unveil their genius — what they know about who they are and what they came here to express. Those around them can shine a light on their brilliance, magnifying it and inviting it into full expression, or dim their light, forcing their gifts into the shadows.

Remember How Clear You Used to Be

Clarity about passion and purpose fade when you're encouraged to disconnect from *child's play,* adapt to the pressures of *real life*, and get in step with what it means to mature.

You turn away from your Spirit and acquiesce to the demands of *The Border Patrol* and its insistence that you be *realistic.* The inner light that once glowed brightly dims or is switched off. Your knowledge of your deeper, true Self recedes and eventually fades away. You become a responsible, functional adult; practical, squarely facing life. You're left with only a faint recall of the once grand sense you had of yourself and what you thought you might become.

Think back to when you were a child, before the restrictive influences took hold and recast your conception of yourself. Most probably, you were once as clear and confident as Kamryn. You knew you were great at many things; born to be a superstar. Perhaps, like Lee, you knew exactly what intrigued you. *That knowledge still resides in you. Your passion, which is your Purpose, calls for attention and expression.* After all, it's what you're here to do. When you embrace and live your Purpose, you'll feel energized and fulfilled. You're predisposed to feel your best when you are your authentic Self, free of internal barriers and blocks.

The certainty of your genius endures! Genius and Purpose – they're one and the same and *cannot* be extinguished. Your brilliance, and the talents you need to fulfill your Purpose, can only be covered over, temporarily denied, discouraged for a while. Their expression is truncated until you make the deliberate choice to allow your brilliant light to shine again.

Every step you take to release the LIES in your life leads you closer to living with a Spirit of Purpose; your energy and intention focused on being who you really are instead of who you have been told you are. The difference between the two may be dramatic.

Sitting in the Soup

Without a doubt, we benefit from most of the lessons of early life. And, many of us are still plagued by unintended lessons conveyed by well-meaning people, who loved us and wanted the best for us. It's as if all that's in our environment is an invisible soup. We sit in it, soaking up the flavors around us — those that help us experience the sweetness of life and the satisfaction of dreams fulfilled, and those that leave a bitter taste in our mouth or leave us hungry for something more fulfilling. Such was the case with Rob.

In a coaching session, Rob shared some of his story. "Mom made a lot of sacrifices to raise and educate me. I'm grateful for that. She taught me many things that have served me well, but she also passed on her fears and tendency to worry. On a daily basis, she acquainted and reacquainted me with the *realities* of life."

Rob was afraid to take risks despite his success. He carries the same worries as his mother who was afraid to do anything that might jeopardize their security. For Rob, fear, like most LIES, was passed on from one generation to the next.

Though no longer relevant, the habit of restraint and worry remained rooted in him, slowing his agility as a decision-maker and inhibiting his willingness to take even calculated risk. It also robbed him of peace of mind.

Most parents and guardians sincerely attempt to raise their children well. They offer all the love, guidance, and protection they can. Values are instilled. Family stories and traditions are passed on. Lessons are taught about the best way to survive, sometimes through words, and mostly by example or invisible means. We learn the lessons by virtue of being in the environment; it's the soup in which we sit.

We sit in the cultural and environmental soup, soaking up the tastes and texture of everyone and everything around us. Imprinted by our experiences, like a snapshot, we develop a fixed and frozen image of who we are and who we are not. The story of you sets and is enlarged as it is told and reinforced by those around you. Hearing the same comments over and over, they begin to sound descriptive and factual. Other people — important others — tell you the story of who you are.

- "You're so smart."
- "You're lazy. You just won't work hard or apply yourself to anything."

- "You're such a good student."
- "You won't listen. You're hard-headed."
- "You're always misbehaving."
- "How do you think you're going to make a living doing *that?*"
- "You're wasting your time dreaming about a Hollywood career."
- "You're rude and insensitive."
- "You're too sensitive."
- "You let people walk all over you. You're not tough enough."
- "You're clumsy and careless. You'd trip over your own feet."

Convinced of the constantly reinforced story, you agree and live into it, feeling as if you have no choice. They've told you, "*This* is who you are." You're stuck in a story — one you didn't consciously write.

Words, Deeds, Images, and Energy

LIES are taught through words, deeds, images, and energy. Messages come from everywhere: from parents and caretakers, family and community members, siblings, playmates and classmates, books, movies, and religious and social institutions, including the educational system.

Frequent repetition of the message — the Label, Illusion, Excuse, or Story — strengthens its controlling power. The more credible the messenger, the stronger the emotional imprint. When the messenger has some level of authority or a perceived position of power over us, the LIES are even more firmly fixed in our psyche. Their roots go deep down into our belief system — so deep they operate outside of our awareness.

The most powerful messages are almost never explicitly taught or spoken. They are projected through invisible transmission — an energetic, emotional exchange. No one has to say a word; you just feel the meaning. You get the message. Unspoken lessons are the most potent because they're conveyed through emotion. Feelings are more powerful than words.

Alice's story is an example. Transmitted through the energy her mother conveyed when they encountered others, her mother taught her with whom she could be at ease and of whom she should be afraid.

"Mom always held my hand when we were in public places. If we were in an elevator, a parking garage, walking down the street or waiting for a table in a restaurant, her touch would change depending on who was nearby or approaching. If it was another woman, she was usually at ease. If it was a white man, dressed in business attire, or casual and clean, she also seemed comfortable. But, if a black man, or a man who didn't look like our family, neighbors and friends approached, she would forcibly pull me closer, positioning me in front of her, with both hands on my shoulders. That sent a message to me, a message I'll never forget."

I asked her about family discussions concerning race and class. Her response was not surprising.

"Oh, God. My family is liberal and believes in equality. We were taught to respect everyone and treat all people the same."

But, actions speak louder than words, and the emotional energy conveyed is the most impactful component. When we say one thing and do another, what's more trustworthy is the feeling communicated through the actions. The more palpable and emotionally charged the energy, the more deeply embedded the roots.

Concerning their children, people say, "I don't know where she learned that." Or, "No one taught him that." Well, that may be true in the sense that no one sat with him and verbally communicated the message. But, the information was transmitted through the most powerful form of communication – through the energy and emotions that live within and between words – through nonverbal communication.

My brother, Lee, and I often laugh about our mother's ability to send a clear directive through her eyes and body language. She didn't have to say a word. All she had to do was look at us from the choir stand, across the room, or the dinner table. We knew what the look meant. Carrying the power to change behavior every time, no question, it was transformative communication.

Along with "the look," Mom had another tool: tone of voice. Subtle variations in her tone would speak volumes. She could say the same words, like calling our names, and depending on the tone, the meaning would be different. We knew the difference between her simply trying to get our attention and when we were "in trouble." It was all in the way her voice sounded.

Children learn how to read nonverbal signals from the time they're in the womb. You have to be able to read the vibes, the energy, and the emotional tone of other people *and* places. It helps you make decisions that ensure safety and the appropriate action or reaction. This same energy is how many Labels, Illusions, Excuses, and Stories are communicated and instilled.

Sometimes a child is called stupid, hard-headed, shy, or stubborn. The words and their energy have an impact. They tell a story about who *they* think we are and what *they* believe we're capable of. The energy of the exchange conveys an image of how we're seen and regarded, whether we're loved and cherished. Words will mean little if they aren't congruent with the invisible emotional current of the exchange.

Journal Your Truth

Remember when you were bold and full of confidence.
- *What excited you?*
- *What were you passionate about?*
- *What did you imagine you were born to do?*
- *What did you tell others you were going to be when you grew up?*

Remember how alive you felt? Do you still feel that way? If not, why not?

Remember when you were unambiguous.
- *What did you love doing?*
- *What were your favorite games and activities?*
- *What roles did you take on naturally, at your own initiation? Were you a police officer, a cowboy or cowgirl, a nurse, a hairdresser, the mom, the dad, an astronaut, a banker, a baker, a person of the clergy, a generous rich person, a business owner, a beach bum, a sailor, or the President?*

What image of yourself did you develop as a result of the soup in which you sat?

Chapter Three

Pivot Points

❦

Moments of Life-Defining Choice

Just about everyone's development is arrested at a critical, pivotal point. Like a snapshot, their self-image is frozen in time. We all live with beliefs about life and ourselves that *seem true* but are *not truth*. Borne out of misunderstandings, LIES lead to the development of lasting mental models – ways of thinking – and unconscious habits. Lost in LIES, you lose connection with your deeper Self and travel the same territory, over and over again, unable to find a way out – a closed loop is established.

This closed-loop can only be interrupted when you allow for the possibility of other interpretations. Since most people are invested in the LIES they live, creating such an opening can be a challenge. When an opening occurs, the moment, not unlike the one that led to the current understanding, is magical and transformational. It is a *Pivot Point* – a time when a change of mind can lead to a change in direction toward the light of deeper self-awareness and positive action or toward the dark shadows of self-destructive alternatives.

Movement toward one direction or another is up to the individual, though it's seldom seen that way. *Pivot Points* are moments of life-defining choice – be it made consciously or unconsciously.

Your Story and Pivot Points

Everyone is affected by what happens in his or her life, particularly early on. No one escapes that reality. Much of my work involves helping people decipher the *Pivot Points* in their story – the particular moments and situations that determined the direction of their development, making them the person they know.

Pivot Points are the significant events that occur in your life. Whether clear and observable or subtle and barely noticeable, *Pivot Points* orient our focus in a particular direction, depending on the story we build around the meaning of the event. Out of all the stimulation in your life, why a particular circumstance becomes your focus is hard to say. The fact is for some reason, that situation impressed you, planting an emotional energy seed that grew roots.

Determinants of the way we think, feel, and behave are imperceptible, long-forgotten memories that can escape our attention entirely. Yet, whether they are obvious, barely detectable, or fully outside of our awareness, the effects of *Pivot Points* determine the direction of our life, stimulate specific feelings, and define every decision we make and every action we take. *Pivot Points* can have an affirming effect or they can hinder us.

We can point to certain experiences and identify the impact they had on us. Their effect is readily apparent. For example, at 52 years old, Della still resists speaking to strangers, let alone making presentations. She stuttered as a child and remembers the ridicule and feelings of humiliation she experienced. While she hasn't stuttered in nearly forty years, she remains terrified of speaking publicly. The terrorist within – her fear-filled memory guarded by *The Border Patrol* – holds her back professionally and robs her of the confidence she deserves.

Della has a tangible explanation – discomfort. If you can explain why you like one thing or fear another, based on "what happened to you when," you're probably describing an obvious and effective *Pivot Point*.

When a shaper is more elusive, or totally outside of our awareness, it leaves you wondering, "What happened? How and why did I get to be this way?" That was Mark's situation.

A financial disaster, in debt up to his eyeballs and still spending, Mark's mantra was, "I don't know how this happened." Uncovering the *Pivot Point* that set up this dynamic required serious investigative work.

Mark resented having to provide for himself. From the time he was a child, he wanted to be taken care of. Unlike his friends, his parents were unable to afford a life of comforts. Hard working, they didn't always have enough to make ends meet.

Honest about his feelings, he said, "I resented the way we lived. No one was as poor as we were. Instead of playing like a kid should, I was working to have lunch money. No kid should be forced to do that."

Frequently, Mark went lacking and that outraged him. It wasn't until he was an adult that he managed to get even. He placed himself in a position to file for bankruptcy. Finally, he was taken care of, relieved of debt and obligations. At last, he didn't have to be self-responsible for his lifestyle. Someone else paid.

For Mark, like many people, the impact of *Pivot Points* is unconscious. Only by uncovering the emotional root of his ongoing financial problems did he find the hidden, rageful attitude and hardened beliefs that guided his daily behavior and created his current financial circumstances. Finally, he understood "how this happened." He made it happen. Without self-examination, he could have assumed it was just the situation, the economy, or an unfortunate turn of events.

Based on the particulars of your life experience, spoken and unspoken messages received, images you saw, and what you witnessed happening to others, many influences converge to create the *Pivot Points* and LIES that impact your life. Each individual involved in any situation translates the inputs received into a specific story, the outcome of which carries only a hint of predictability. The stimulus that feels like love to one person is thought to be intrusive to another and overwhelming to a third. No one can determine exactly how anything will land and rest in the heart and mind of another.

What's the proof of that? Siblings. Ask any set, same gender or different, and you'll uncover the story of people who took different turns based on the same event. One may experience the event and make a left turn, the other may turn right, another may do an about-face, and yet another may stand still, unaffected. Two siblings who experience the same *Pivot Points* will likely remember them differently and attribute different meaning to them. Fact is, the *Pivot Point* is the same, but what it means to one versus the other is specific to the person and how he or she positions the story they carry about who they are.

The Pivot Point Process

The *Pivot Point* process begins with an event that is interpreted in a particular way and that interpretation, accurate or false, becomes fact. The process operates in this way:

1. You experience something.
2. You decide what it means and assume the meaning you've assigned is accurate.
3. Taking root in your thoughts and emotions, interpretation sets. You're certain that what you believe about the event is indisputable fact.
4. You use future experiences to validate your belief.
5. A vicious cycle is established and you are *lost in LIES*.
6. Your LIES become *true*, *reality*, and determine future actions and reactions.
7. Fixed and frozen, your mindset – thoughts and feelings – don't allow you to see the situation differently or mature beyond it. The rut deepens. Development is arrested. Evolution is short-circuited.

Sometimes the *Pivot Point* process works obviously and predictably. At other times, it happens mysteriously and outside our awareness. In either case, when *Pivot Points* occur, you interpret the event, determining its meaning based on:

- What you **think** about it.
- And more powerfully and important, how you *feel* about it.

As you assess the situation, thoughts and questions that cross your mind may include:

- "How do I feel about this?"
- "I like this." Or, "I don't like this."
- "I want this." Or, "I don't want that."

- "This is what happens to people who..."
- "He did/didn't deserve that."
- "Will this happen to me in this way?"
- "I feel (mad, glad, sad, scared, loving)."

Sometimes, as these questions occur, you carefully think them through and make a decision. Most often, however, they're not consciously considered. These questions occur in an indistinguishable flash that is seemingly simultaneous to the experience. The *Pivot Point* process runs like a background program – functioning outside of awareness, yet defining the pattern of possibilities.

Everything in your life has the potential to shape you in one direction or another, even one-time events and situations to which you consciously pay little to no attention. *Pivot Points* set up guiding assumptions and core values, some of which affirm and support the truth of who you are and some that limit your life.

When we witness children prophesying or acting out their dreams, we're in the midst of an important moment – a *Pivot Point*. How the listeners and observers respond is important. The words we speak and the energy and meaning the child receives determine if he feels his dream is received or rejected by the listener. In either case, the listener's reaction can set up a *Pivot Point*, as illustrated by Mani's story.

A Doctor for Everyone...A Dream Dismissed

Mani grew up in a village outside of Chennai, in south India. As a child, he loved playing "doctor," helping the sick and lame.

"My siblings and the neighborhood kids were my patients. I treated their afflictions, prescribing medication and therapeutic regimes. Even my parents and grandparents had their turn in my examination room or on the operating table. I was doctor to everyone."

The fifth of eight children, Mani's parents indulged play but encouraged him to "find a more suitable career, something less academically rigorous." He, in their judgment, did not have his oldest brother's intellectual capacity.

Fearing he would fail, they steered him away from medicine "for his own good."

For whose good was that, again? Certainly, not Mani's. This well-intended directive drove Mani's career choice. Twenty years later, he's still angry with his parents for their lack of faith and encouragement, and jealous of his brother who had full parental support. Guided away from his passionate interest and natural gifts — medicine and healing — and toward a field in which his parents believed he could succeed, Mani became an accountant.

Many people have compromised and been traitor to their talents and gifts. Giving in to familial or social pressure, they oriented their lives away from what they loved and toward something that was a forced fit. It's a deadening choice for most, as it was for Mani.

When we met, Mani was not well thought of by his organization. Passed over for promotions and developmental assignments, his performance was average. Judged as not particularly talented, he was labeled lazy and lacking ambition. His management was right. Accounting didn't really interest him. His passion, talents, and ambition were not aligned with the work he was educated and paid to do.

Bored and deeply dissatisfied, Mani was faced with a choice. He could continue to do work that did not satisfy him. Or, he could design a path that would lead him to what he loved. Becoming a medical doctor was still a possibility. Nursing, emergency medical technician, physician's assistant, chiropractic medicine, energy medicine, and more were all viable possibilities. Choices abound. But, as of this writing, Mani is still an unhappy, unmotivated, average accountant. He has refused to *pivot* in favor of a more fulfilling work life.

Like Mani, we also paralyze ourselves with the fear of change. Even when it could move us closer to a lifelong goal, we view change as a risk. We don't consider the hazardous consequences involved in remaining in a place that robs us of our life force and the opportunity to allow our God-given gifts to manifest. We don't take seriously the price we pay in terms of emotional well-being and physical health when we live a life devoid of living our unique purpose. Ignoring the idea that he is his own worst enemy, Mani has sentenced himself to a life of dull tedium, doing work that he doesn't enjoy when what he does love is so clear. He is the thief who has stolen his vitality.

The Border Patrol, that mental menace, continues to have full authority over Mani. He's afraid to step outside the boundaries defined by past familial pressures, despite his resentment of the limits they establish. He is living LIES, denying his passion and potential.

Journal Your Truth

Think back to your childhood.
- *Who were your primary teachers?*
- *What story were you told about your capability?*
- *What limits did people around you set on your options and potential?*
  - *Parents?*
  - *Other family members?*
  - *Teachers?*
  - *Neighbors?*
  - *Friends and peers?*
  - *The broader society?*

What have been key Pivot Points in your life?

Which messages and lessons stay with you:
- *Words spoken?*
- *Deeds done?*
- *Images imprinted?*
- *Energy transmitted?*

Which Pivot Points directed you positively?

Which Pivot Points have hampered your choices and growth?

Like Mani, with what are you dissatisfied and disillusioned?

Chapter Four

Choices and Consequences

☙❧

How Pivot Points Affect a Life

The *Pivot Points* in your life establish the filters through which you make selections and experience the consequences of your choices. That's true of causal factors we can identify and describe, and equally true of factors whose effects we see as we examine our preferences, actions, and the patterns in our lives.

Notice the obvious, subtle, and invisible ways *Pivot Points* oriented Joe's thinking. Examine the ways beliefs were implanted without his conscious awareness – beliefs that were inconsistent with his intentions.

A successful marketing executive, Joe wondered, "Why can't I build and sustain a love relationship? In my professional life, I thrive. But, when it comes to women and intimate relationships, I might as well be the tin man. I just can't seem to make it work, at least not for long."

Easy to talk with, Joe had an active sense of humor and told engaging stories. He was 6'2", about 210 pounds, and easy on the eyes. Factors that led to his success were obvious and easily recounted.

"I grew up in a working-class family where there was not enough money for necessities. From the time I was fifteen, I was independent, working and able to take care of myself, and even helping my family."

Playing football and basketball, Joe honed the competitive side of his personality. He excelled academically and was awarded a scholarship to college. There, he also performed well.

That's the easy and obvious part of his story. In it, you can see the *Pivot Points*, the central conditions in his life, and how they drove him in the direction of hard worker and high achiever.

But what about this dangling and disturbing issue of his relationships with women? This part of the picture was perplexing. It forced him to look more deeply, exploring the forgotten, shadowy corners of his experiences and calling out the unconscious meaning he made of some important life events.

When you recollect *Pivot Points* in your history, inevitably they reveal secrets that allow you to know more about what was not previously in the realm of your conscious awareness.

For most people with whom I've worked, the answers to the mysteries in their lives are in the stories and metaphors they use. The images conjured up by the selected figure of speech is always telling. Such was true of Joe's statement, "When it comes to women and intimate relationships, I might as well be the tin man."

The eldest of two children, and the first-born grandchild on both sides of the family, Joe was joyfully anticipated. After his birth, Joe's mother became depressed. His care reverted to his maternal grandmother. His mother seldom held him, fed him, or changed his diaper.

Though she recovered from depression, Joe said, "She was never herself again."

He described what he called, "...the vacant look in her eyes," and how "...she felt hollow, like she wasn't really alive, like I couldn't really touch *her*."

Here was a man who lived his entire life feeling the absence of his mother. He was just an infant when it happened, but what he took from the situation was life altering. He told himself, well beneath his awareness, that he was unlovable. His view of this *Pivot Point*, which wasn't truth, took root in his emotional belief system. The label stuck. The reality of his being – lovable because you exist – was denied. LIES prevailed.

This particular illusion, "I am unlovable," cast a dark shadow on his relationships. He wasn't cognizant of the specific LIES that limited his ability to have and enjoy what he consciously believed he desired and deserved. Not knowing it, he feared being able to meet or match the emotional energy of women he found appealing.

"Look," he said, "to be honest, I don't know if I have the capacity to love her back, to be that vulnerable and open."

Privately, Joe worried and shamed himself. "I feel empty. Maybe I really am the tin man." He laughed nervously, uncomfortable with this tender place. He frightened himself with the aliveness and available hearts of the women who moved through his life. More deeply, he feared rejection was inevitable.

He questioned, "What if they find out about the real me? What then? They're not going to love a guy who can't love them back." He no longer remembered the truth about himself, only his distorted perception – the LIES that caused him to feel unlovable.

For Joe, the development of his most basic human need – to love and to be loved – was thwarted. His openness in this important area was shut down. He now had the job of reclaiming his core essence – his own loving and lovable nature.

Natalie and Natasha: Same Point, Different Directions

Witness the curious power of *Pivot Points* in the lives of twins, Natalie and Natasha. Born just minutes apart, they were raised together, attended the same family and social events, sat in the same classes during school, and shared many of the same friends. Both took piano lessons from the same teacher and participated in the same extracurricular activities. Until they were in middle school, their mother even dressed them alike and gave them identical haircuts.

At the age of fifteen, they experienced the same critical *Pivot Point* – their parents separated and ultimately divorced – but their reactions to that life-changing circumstance took them in different directions. Natalie went forward from the event, her course relatively unaltered. Natasha, however, was changed forever.

"I don't know what happened. When Dad left, I felt lost. I missed him. I guess I substituted the attention of boys for his love. I started to date and became sexually active...really active. I ruined my reputation and embarrassed my family. In a way, I wanted that. I was so angry that dad left me. I wanted to get even. Now I see how much what I did hurt me. I'm so ashamed," Natasha said tearfully.

Natalie shared her experience of the very same *Pivot Point*. "I was sad and embarrassed that our parents split. It wasn't all that common in our little town. I didn't think there was anyone to blame. It just seemed that Mom and Dad couldn't make each other happy. They explained it to us and I accepted what they said. They were not divorcing Natasha and me. Besides, I don't think they could take two of us behaving like Natasha." She smiled at her sister and shook her head.

Natasha continues to work on her need for constant male attention and approval. Fear of abandonment is still a trigger for her. In a very telling moment, she said, "I don't want to be without a man. When I'm in love with a guy, I'll do just about anything to keep him." She has lived up to that statement more than once, and seldom proudly.

While both sisters experienced the same specific event, their parents' separation and divorce, the meaning each made of it was different. That's the perplexing power of *Pivot Points*.

Those Damned Distortions

Children, and many adults, are literal. I favor adjectives, adverbs, images, and metaphors. Being a conceptual thinker and communicator, I listen for what people are *really* saying, tuning in to what is beneath and in-between their words. The limits of spoken language convey only part of what is intended. Deeper meaning is not easily verbalized.

But literal communicators want and need specifics, facts. To them, adjectives, images, and metaphors don't convey clear meaning. Factual and precise communicators want and need to hear descriptive, accurate, tangible details. May's stepdaughter, Amy, was a good teacher in this regard.

When May decided to marry Amy's dad, Amy was ten years old. Understandably, she was reluctant to embrace her new "Mom." One day, while the three of them talked, May turned to Amy and said excitedly, "I want to make a difference in your life."

Amy looked at May and nodded; no words, just the nonverbals. May said, "Her eyes were steady, fixed on me. She was figuring me out, but *not* taking me in."

May continued with her story. "In my eagerness to make the situation work for all of us – to blend and become a happy family – I didn't take the time to slow down and explore how Amy felt about what I said. I saw her leave my words on the table but I didn't ask why. I was too afraid to hear the answer. Instead, I decided I would show her how wonderful living together would be. Then, she would understand what I meant."

How wrong she was! Those well-intended words, "I want to make a difference in your life," were a *Pivot Point* that contributed to many unnecessary years of anguish in their relationship. Why? Amy took May literally, and with a twist – a distortion.

Amy understood May to say, "I'm going to make *you* different." Imagine the hurt and anger that stirred in her. Rejection resulted. Like most people, Amy's natural instinct is self-preservation. Her self-protective reaction was, "No, you're not going to change me."

Someone else might have reacted differently to this *Pivot Point*. Their adaptive response might have led them to say, "I don't understand. What do you mean?" Another person might have felt excited, attracted to the idea. Not Amy. She would have no part of it or of May. She put up a wall, yet to be penetrated.

That's the impact of *Pivot Points*. When an individual experiences something, you never know exactly what meaning they'll make of it. You have an intention, but what the person takes from it, or makes of it, may be something entirely different.

It wasn't until Amy was fourteen that May got a glimpse of the lasting impact of Amy's interpretation of May's words spoken that day in the kitchen, years earlier.

One evening, while the three of them were in the kitchen having dinner, May turned the conversation to their relationship. With a heart-felt desire to open up communication and begin healing the breech, May initiated a conversation.

"Amy, let's talk about our relationship. Neither of us is happy. I'm wondering what would make it better."

Amy blurted, "You don't love me. All you want to do is change me."

May was shocked. Certainly there were aspects of Amy's behavior May didn't like, but this statement was about more than that. "Change you. What do you mean, change you?"

"That's what you said before you married Dad. You said you wanted to make me different."

"Oh, my God!" That was not what May meant. But, it was too late. They couldn't go back and fix it. All these years, Amy believed her child-mind's interpretation. Of course she did. We all do. It doesn't matter that it was a distortion of the intended message. Clearly, it was the emotional root of the strain between them.

What Amy took from that sentence spoken years before guided her every reaction to May. Everything May said or did was vetted through the lens, "May doesn't love me. She wants to change me and I'm not going to let her." With that realization, May opened to new empathy for Amy. You can see how a *Pivot Point* impaired the development of their relationship. Think about it. Would you trust someone who you believe has an objective of making you into a different person?

Pivot Points are powerful. They penetrate the inner recesses of your mind. Because pivotal events are paired with strong, visceral, emotional reactions, they are deeply rooted in your belief system and lay dormant until triggered.

Emotional Roots Anchor Pivot Points

Over the course of my career, I've witnessed much of what happens when a person's emotional maturity is arrested at a particular age. One interesting observation is that the underdeveloped aspect of the individual's personality is frozen in time. Without exaggeration, when the people tap the emotional root of a belief that solidified early in life, they present as the age they were when the *Pivot Point* occurred.

Here's the story of one client with whom I had such an experience.

Les was five years old when his mother moved away to find a better-paying job in another state. She left him with her favorite sister, his favorite aunt.

Lovingly, she explained why she was leaving, where she was going, and when she would return for him. He listened, said, "Okay, Mommy," and ran off to play. He gave no signs, neither then nor later, of any issue with the action she was about to take. She used his externalized reaction to assuage her guilt about leaving him.

Isn't that what we do? We worry about the consequences of an action we are about take. The fact that we are worrying tells us something about it does not feel right. We're not fully aligned with the idea — our head and heart are not in agreement. We talk with the other person about the matter. They say, "Okay," and we say, to ourselves, "What was I worried about!" We're relieved but, we don't know how the other is handling the input, nor what *Pivot Points* will influence their understanding.

In his five-year-old mind, Les made an important, life-defining decision when his mother left, it was a *Pivot Point*. Whenever he talked about the event, his physical appearance changed. He looked, behaved, and felt like a five-year-old. It was as if he traveled back in time and became the little abandoned boy, again.

As Les tells it, "I decided to become a man and be self-sufficient. I did everything myself. I figured out everything. I wanted no one's help with anything. I was angry, but I never showed it. My family bragged about me being such a big boy. I can still see myself, five years old and determined to never need or trust anyone again. Mom's leaving hurt too much."

Today, that decision made by the five-year-old still rules his life. He has very few relationships outside of work. According to him, "None of my relationships are close. I would like to change that, but I don't know how."

He is lonely and bristles at his wife's constant complaint about a lack of emotional intimacy. His pain is based on a misconception, a negative story he told himself long ago. Now, after years of feeling betrayed and abandoned, he is finally at the *emotional root* of a long-standing hurt that crippled his emotional development.

Any event that establishes an *emotional root,* anchors you to that experience. Like time travelers, whenever a similar feeling is stirred, you go right back to the age you were when the *Pivot Point* first occurred — back to the LIES that still limit you.

Ralph's mother died when he was five years old. He said, "I missed her and I was so angry that she left me. I decided to never trust anyone ever again. And, I haven't. But, it's cost me a lot."

Ralph was right. He was guarded in relationships, never relaxing enough to reveal himself to the other person. Without trust, intimacy and the ability to develop lasting and satisfying relationships are impossible.

When he talked about this dimension of his personality, where his right to love was denied, he looked like a five-year-old despite his fifty-plus years. One day, as he talked about his mother's death and how he felt, I asked him, "How old do you feel, right now?" With tears in his eyes, he said, "About five." He was right back there at the moment — the *Pivot Point* — when his heart broke and froze. He held on to that story for much of his life. That's what we do with LIES — we clutch them and guard them as if they are true instead of the LIES they are.

Pivot Points direct us either toward the truth of our strengths, talents, passion, and the call of Spirit, or toward LIES and limits and away from our authentic and powerful Self.

Journal Your Truth

In what ways are you compromising and dampening your life force and the opportunity to express your God-given talents?

Where are you frozen with fear, living under the authority of The Border Patrol?

What price are you paying, in terms of your emotional and physical health?

How many life-defining decisions has the five-year-old in you made?

In what way has your child-mind twisted the meaning of a benign Pivot Point?

Identify one of your Pivot Points.
- *What are the emotional roots that anchor you to it?*
- *How old do you feel when you connect with this Pivot Point?*
- *How has this Pivot Point affected your life?*

Chapter Five

Types of LIES

ejo

Grand Design LIES

Some LIES — Labels, Illusions, Excuses, and Stories — are intentional, deliberately crafted, carefully communicated, and constantly reinforced. I call these distortions the *Grand Design LIES*. Backed by a plan, their existence is conscious and calculated.

Aimed at dominating and subordinating specific groups of people, *Grand Design LIES* are planted by the group that wants control. False beliefs are created — imprinted in the cultural mind — and perpetuated, even by the group the LIES are meant to manage.

A great deal of mass marketing is based on *Grand Design LIES*. They drive our decision-making and behavior. If we want to be in the know, current, cool, a part of the in-group, they tell us how. They tell us what we *should* eat, wear, do, drive, think, value, desire, and devote our energy to. They tell us how to live; how to feel about our bodies; how to feel about other people; the meaning of intimate relationships and how we should behave in them; and they tell us how to view and react to aging, sex, politics, and money. Certainly, they tell us what to buy and how much it's worth.

Ads tell us, women and men, we look old and tired when our gray hair is visible. "Bye, bye gray!"

From the early 1900s through the late 1980s, television commercials and billboards made cigarette smokers attractive. Real, rugged men smoked Marlboro or Camel. Modern, sophisticated women smoked Virginia Slims. Fun-loving young people smoked Kool. Every brand had its image and told us what kind of person we would be if we smoked their brand. Many of us believed them and followed their direction.

We've been told blonde hair and blue eyes are the standard of beauty. Any other color combinations are inferior, less pretty. That image left out many white people and most people of other races. We simply were not as beautiful and desirable. Our hair was the wrong color. "Blondes have more fun," and are more fun. That was the message. I see this story about hair color and eye color as one of the *Grand Design LIES*.

Grand Design LIES permitted masses of people to be enslaved, go to the gas chamber, and die of hunger and thirst in the deserts of Africa. Witnessing such LIES in action, we endure ethnic cleansing. "It's a shame what's happening. Their government is not taking action. What difference can one person make? There's nothing we can do; we can't control them." Said often enough, we convince ourselves we're helpless. Believing the story we're told about our inability to affect the situation, we repeat it. Then, we behave as if what has begun to *sound* true through repetition is actually truth.

"We take care of our own" is a current cultural illusion that sounds right, but is so wrong. It's a narrow-minded way of looking at life and ignoring our interconnectedness and interdependency, locally and globally.

Adolf Hitler told a story that capitalized on a growing distrust and hatred of Jews, making the Holocaust possible. His *Grand Design LIES* vilified and demonized a group of people, making them less human and acceptable than the group creating the LIES about them. Once the perpetrators convinced listeners that *those people* are different from *us* — *they* are not as good or righteous or trustworthy as *we* are — the ground is laid for any atrocity. That's the way it has worked throughout human history.

The same pattern existed with slavery, no matter the group being enslaved. The slavery of millions of people of African descent was established, rationalized, and perpetuated in the United States. The basis was simple: *they* are not like *us*. In fact, *they* are less than human. *We* are the real humans, smarter and closer to God. God favors us. Labeled nigger, monkeys, animals, the illusion that allowed for the enslavement of black people was perpetuated. The good Christian slave owners assuaged their guilt with the excuse that Negroes needed to be owned and taken care of. They were providing a service to the ignorant and child-like. This is the way *Grand Design LIES* work.

Belief in any ism – racism, sexism, classism, heterosexism, nationalism, ageism – means you're succumbing to *Grand Design LIES*. Buying in to any sweeping statement that sounds like *we* are better than *they* are or *our way* is right and *their way* is wrong is tantamount to perpetuating the limiting Labels, Illusions, Excuses, and Stories in grand design proportions. No matter the group holding the idea, this way of seeing others is based on misconceptions and imposes false distinctions.

LIES We Speak Every Day

LIES – Labels, Illusions, Excuses, and Stories – set up erroneous assumptions and false limits, undermining your belief that you have options and change is within your grasp. LIES challenge your ability to dream big, or at all. Knowing how to look and listen for LIES is the first step toward addressing them.

Here are some clues to or cues that reveal common, everyday LIES that manifest through the way we think and speak. Too frequently, I have made these statements, believing them, speaking them as if they were truth. Placing faith in them, I made them my reality. Each statement below represents a culturally accepted mindset and tees up Labels, Illusions, Excuses, and Stories – the restrictive consequences of which you and I live with:

- *I can't, because…*
- *But, I don't know how to…*
- *They won't let someone like me…*
- *I don't have time to…*
- *Everybody [feels, thinks, is] that way.*
- *Everybody does…sometime. Right?*
- *Not now. I'll do it later, once…*
- *When…happens, then I'll be able to…*
- *When the kids are older, I'll…*
- *When I'm older, I'll…*
- *That kind of [good, wonderful] thing happens to other people, not me.*
- *Nobody in my [family, neighborhood, school, racial or ethnic group] has ever…*

These statements are well rehearsed LIES, misconceptions that disable the believer and anyone who speaks them readily. Hearing them from others, you may find yourself responding as if the person was sharing accurate, unquestionable information. By tolerating the presence of these life-limiting LIES, you affirm and validate them. Believing them without thought, you make them your reality. But they are merely long-accepted ways of thinking and talking, LIES we speak every day that can be challenged and changed.

LIES About Reality

Like the LIES we speak every day, we have other ideas about reality that seem equally solid and unquestionable. Here are a few examples. Consider the degree to which they've influenced your perceptions, decision-making, and actions.

- *I can't get over <u>this</u>. I can't let <u>that</u> go. I can't forgive [<u>him</u>, <u>her</u>, <u>them</u>].* The truth is you can get over anything, IF you're willing to forgive and move forward. It's not that you can't, you're just unwilling; perhaps you are more invested in holding on to rage and resentment than you are in being released from the grip of the situation.
- *People can't really change; it's too hard.* Change is hard because we fight it; we resist flowing with our lives. Instead we hold on tightly to what is, or in many cases, what was. We're far behind the place where Spirit resides and calls us to. Keeping up with our ever-evolving Self is easy if we let go of our grip on the past and flow toward what's calling us. We have to learn to say YES with our minds and hearts, talk ourselves into changing. We'll talk more about how to do this when we discuss "Aligning Your Energy and Intentions."
- *An education guarantees you a good life.* Education is desirable and helpful. It can broaden and deepen your capacity to think critically and expand your knowledge. But, nothing guarantees you a good life except YOU and the energy and intentions – the feelings and thoughts – you use to create every part of your precious life.

- *If I had the money, I would…* It is almost always an excuse, a way of letting yourself off the hook, not being fully accountable. There are always conditions to deal with and it's critical to call yourself to task, to do an integrity check. See if your *IF* is a legitimate statement of unknown probability or an easy out because you're unwilling to do the work or take the risk involved in doing what you imagine money makes possible. Some people live very well with very little money. What's really holding you back?

- *I'm not ready for that [position, relationship, change in my life].* Sometimes it's true that you're not ready. Usually the people who are not ready don't know it. They say yes to the opportunity and then find a way to succeed. Or they don't grow into it and muddle through or move on to something else. Those who have the awareness to say they're not ready usually mean, "I'm scared. I can't see myself doing that. I'm not willing to take the risk. I'm not motivated enough to do the work required to figure it out."

- *I'm ready to…, but…* What's your but? But usually means you're not going to move, you're going to remain where you are, sitting on your butt. If you're ready to, begin moving. Baby steps are better than but, and in Chapter Eight, you'll read about a concept I call *Tick-Talk, Tick-Talk*. It's one of the biggest ways we waste time and energy. This sentiment, "I'm ready to…, but…" is one of the ways we remain glued to what we don't want.

- *Life is hard. There are so many roadblocks and hurdles.* There can be roadblocks and hurdles, but they need not stop us from pursuing our passion and aligning with the energy of Spirit. Look at roadblocks and hurdles as feedback. If a lot of them are appearing along your path, investigate two questions: First, "Am I on the right road?" Second, "How am I, through the way I'm thinking and feeling, creating or contributing to the existence of these roadblocks?" Your first tendency may be to not see your part in the problems and obstacles that show up. Don't worry; you're not alone. To work through your blindness ask yourself, with the full integrity of an open heart and mind, to see your role in the challenges and most assuredly, the answer will come.

- *It's too late for me to...* If you say it is, it is. This is all about the way you see things. I know a woman who decided at 60 to go to medical school. She had always wanted to be a physician. Most would say it was too late. She chose not to be limited by convention; she decided not to allow LIES to rule her life. You can too.

- *If I work hard and keep my nose clean, I'll get what I deserve.* I talk more about LIES of this nature in the chapter on "LIES Detector Tools." Your experience has probably taught you a thing or two about this common belief and mantra. Surely you've witnessed what appear to be the unjust rewards that come to those who keep their heads down and their noses clean expecting their good work to speak for them. For now, know this: hard work merely sets the foundation for the house you want to build. Much more is involved in constructing, furnishing, and finishing the home of your dreams.

- *I can't let him/them know how I <u>really</u> feel. Vulnerability is dangerous.* LIES like this keep us well defended and trapped in silent suffering. Of all the hurt inflicted, we hurt ourselves more than anyone else. Besides, what you feel seeps out of the edges. So much is transmitted nonverbally*, energetically*; remember? We talked about that in Chapter Three — *Pivot Points*. And, saying how you really feel is a skill you can develop. The main objective is to be clear about what you feel and describe the impact a situation has had on you. When you learn to say how you feel without blaming others, threatening them, or putting them down — in other words, not making them wrong — you will have mastered the ability to say anything to anyone. This is a skill set worth the work of developing. You'll be a masterful communicator.

- *This is the way it <u>should</u> be done. Should* is a statement of expectations that says my way is the right way, the only way. That is never true. You may have preferences, in which case you can express what you prefer. *Should* limits options and halts creativity and expansive thinking. It establishes exclusionary conditions. Is that what you want? In some cases, for very specific reasons, perhaps so. But as we craft our lives, *shoulds* set up too many constraints that don't serve our development and freedom of expression.

- *Fear is natural. Everyone is afraid to...* Because it's so prevalent, fear feels natural and normal. Yet, I wonder about that. Does it have to be so present, palpable, and pervasive? I certainly don't want fear ruling my life. Here's something to consider: the real you is not afraid, not ever. In your core is a calm, still presence that is collected and grounded under the most terrifying conditions. It's that voice that says, "Cross the street." "Take this route today." "Get off at this exit." "Don't resign." "It's time to move on." "Say yes." "Go." "Stay." It's the voice that tells you what to do in important situations, in emergencies, at times of need. Notice how nonjudgmental, clear, and direct its instructions are. Its message is clear because its observations are not clouded or paralyzed by fear. Learn to listen to and trust this part of you. This is your fearless Spirit speaking.

- *My private thoughts don't hurt anyone. Only my actions that others know about can be harmful.* It's always interesting to me how many people say, "I had a feeling she was having an affair." Or, "I knew I shouldn't have agreed to the contract." We know these things because we are always transmitting energy that's received and read by others. Our secret thoughts are not so secret. The reason we're not challenged more about the things we keep secret is because most people don't trust their feelings and intuition. So, our private thoughts and feelings affect our relationships whether we simply feel the other person withdraw a bit more or we withhold because something in our gut tells us to be watchful. Private thoughts of a negative nature do harm because they are felt, even if they're not named or confronted. We get that something isn't right, though we may not act on it.

- *When you're dead, you're done.* This illusion is shared my many. I differ, believing death is simply a transition from one form of energetic expression to another. We're never done. As Einstein taught us, energy can neither be created nor destroyed. Though not in the body we know today, we exist forever as Spirit, which is energy.

- *You learn from your mistakes.* This is certainly true. And, we can also learn from our successes. Few of us take the time to analyze successes. What a joy to answer the question, "What did I do that made that work so brilliantly?" We spend more time talking about and dissecting results that didn't match expectations. What if you, your family, teams you work with — what if we all spent at least as much time analyzing our successes as we do our "mistakes"? Both mistakes and successes are feedback, about the action-consequence sequence, and are a gold mine of insights for growth.

LIES Are Outdated Beliefs

Repeated often — by others and through your self-talk — LIES sound true. If something is said frequently enough and with emotional force, we begin to assume it must be right. That's what happens with LIES in our lives. Repeated with frequency and force, even the most ridiculous thing starts to sound accurate despite evidence to the contrary. We'll ignore the evidence and our own good sense, in favor of the popular story.

Many LIES are simply misguided, outdated beliefs or ways of being that were once valid, but are no longer. In such instances, what was a temporary survival tactic becomes *the* way to be. It just feels right and comfortable.

A brilliant African-American man, Adam was quiet and reserved, not a fit for the verbal sparring characteristic of his colleagues on the senior leadership team.

Exploring the issue, Adam told me, "*They* don't see me as their equal."

"*They* don't," I replied. "Why do you think that's so?" I was very interested in his response.

"Because I'm black. White people don't see black people as their equal." He made his point as if I *should* have known.

"Never mind what *they* think. Do *you* feel you're their equal?" I asked, pointing to the center of my chest, indicating the place from which I wanted him to respond. I was going for depth of feeling, not well-rehearsed top-of-mind thought.

"I *know* I'm their equal. I had to be twice as good to get here."

He dodged my question. I wasn't asking about his intellectual assessment of the situation, nor did I want to hear the story about why and how he had risen to his current, impressive position. I was asking a deeper, more important question. I wanted to know if he *felt* equal. His reluctant response suggested he had historical, race-based baggage that was affecting his sense of himself with this group.

Was the group racist, even slightly? Maybe. Maybe not. That wasn't the issue. Our task was to *unshackle him* from the *LIES* that limited him. His goal was to *be* their equal – in his head and heart – regardless of his colleagues' attitudes, beliefs, or behaviors.

Adam peeled back the layers of his story about his place within this group, and his place in the world as a black man. It's not as if he took an aspirin and the pain was gone. His work was and is way more significant than that. It takes constant vigilance on his part, to this day. Adam has to be self-aware, noticing what he's thinking, how he's feeling, and how he's choosing to behave, every day – without regard for what others are saying and doing. This ensures his independence from the constraints of LIES.

Adam's job, like yours and mine, is to *make conscious choices* that support his personal power and well-being and honor his immense gifts and talents. We are whole when we are in harmony with all parts of our Selves – body, mind, emotions, Spirit, and Purpose.

Journal Your Truth

Put a check mark next to the list of LIES you speak every day, on page 45.

How do these statements serve or benefit you?

What negative impact do LIES have on your day-to-day behavior and life?

List some examples of Grand Design LIES that have shaped your beliefs?

Which Grand Design LIES have you perpetuated?

Which generalizations or isms have you spoken as truth?
- *Men / Women are...*
- *Whites / Blacks / Asians / Hispanics are...*
- *Americans / Islamic people / Europeans are...*
- *Terrorists are...*
- *Rich people / Poor people are..., etc.*
- *Gays / Lesbians / Transsexuals are...*
- *Fat people are...*
- *Southerners / Northerners are...*
- *Lawyers are... / Garbage men are..., etc.*

Which of your ideas about reality will you begin to challenge?

What thoughts and feelings do you hold on to that are no longer relevant?

Which of your beliefs are outdated?

Where might you make a conscious choice that honors your gifts and personal power?

Chapter Six

How LIES Become A Part of You

❦

Mind-Training

Mind-training is helpful, it allows us to know the rules and cultural norms — what it takes to survive in our environment. The rules and norms make life with the collective orderly and reasonably predictable. We have a shared understanding of symbols and act according to expectations for various settings. That's good; we want that.

We expect other drivers to stop when the light is red. We want our fellow citizens to wait their turn in line. We want the people in our intimate circle to be trustworthy and not harm us as we sleep or take advantage of our tender vulnerabilities. We want certain aspects of life to be predictable. When that occurs we feel safe. But, sometimes we take a good thing too far.

The social rules and expectations can be unnecessarily restrictive and inhibit awareness and use of one's full potential. That's when the rules we live by are used against us.

For example, most of us have been raised to be polite and to play nicely with others. This is appropriate until it interferes with your ability to give and receive feedback constructively or to respectfully offer a difference of opinion, when warranted. Or, you may live by the creed "don't brag on yourself." That's a good thing until it renders you mute concerning the impact of your particular contribution to a project's success. Taken to extreme, this culturally sanctioned idea can become career limiting.

If you don't want to say no or hurt anyone's feelings, you probably spend a great deal of time denying *your* real feelings and preferences in favor of keeping the peace, making others happy, smoothing things over, going along to get along. But, whose peace is kept? Certainly not yours, and probably not that of the others involved. Who is happy? Not you and most likely not the other people either because they probably know you are insincere and disingenuous. So, with whom are you getting along? Not with yourself nor anyone else, not really. The real you is not there.

Without the real you saying yes, or feeling peaceful or happy, there is no integrity in the interaction. Without integrity, your truth is denied, your principles compromised, your sense of worth diminished. Stymieing your contribution to yourself and others, you are unintentionally less than who you really are.

Social standards for how you *should* think, how you *should* feel, and what you *should* do too often take precedence over your truth and dreams. You end up living in a way that pleases others more than yourself. Loyal to a pattern of thought and action that once served you, but now, no longer suits you. You feel unable to break free. The cost of change seems too high. The outcome of moving contrary to convention feels too risky and uncertain. Sabotaging your willingness and ability to fully govern your life and shape it according to your calling and dreams, you succumb to faulty beliefs.

No matter our level of outward success, there is a place in most of us where we are imprisoned by constraints. These are the places in our minds where we are not free to honor our longing. The power of our programming — the explicit and implicit messages about what we can and can't do — feels stronger than our will to change. Furthermore, we are not always clear that the need for change rests with us. We too easily imagine it's the others in the world — other people, the company, the government — that should change. Feeling helpless when we're unable to convince them to change, we pretend we've resigned our grievance and accepted what is. But the complaints continue, even if the muttering is never uttered to another.

"Marry a Teacher, Don't Become One": A Dream Discounted

From his earliest recollections, Woody says, "I wanted to be a teacher. I thought there was nothing more noble and important. Knowledge is a door to another dimension. Even when I was little, I knew the more education I had, the more respected I would be, and more capable of helping others."

Coming from a struggling, working-class background, his parents were happy about his love of learning. To them, education was the way up the socioeconomic ladder.

When it came time to talk careers, Woody made it clear he wanted to be a social studies teacher. But, his parents wanted their son to be a businessman, like Mr. Sanzoto who ran the corner insurance agency.

"They used to say to me, 'You have such a good head on your shoulders. Be a businessman. You'll make more money. Marry a teacher, don't become one.' I'll never forget that."

How could he forget that! His dreams were discounted with the words of one sentence: "Marry a teacher, don't become one."

The Focus on Money

Woody is not alone. Many of us have had our dreams dismissed through other's negative reaction to our passion. Absent their support and encouragement, you go along with *their* idea of what *you should* do with *your* life. Your talents and where you might fit best are not a consideration. Their coaching emphasizes how and where you *should* focus your efforts to earn enough money. The information doesn't guide you toward using your talents to make a contribution <u>and</u> a living.

Unintentionally, much of their good advice provides excellent direction on how to become a wage slave – a person who works strictly for money, with no thought of doing work that aligns with their sense of mission and purpose; work that would allow them to contribute to others, using their natural gifts and talents, and make a decent living.

We put money before our Spirit and Purpose. It becomes our god and guide to which we give our lifeblood. Funny thing, no matter how much of it you get, it is never enough. Money is an insatiable false god. A unique aspect of *The Border Patrol,* money has been used as a tool of control since its invention. We choose to love and quest after money more readily than we choose to love and quest after a relationship with our Selves.

Some of us act as if a specific job is above or beneath us, or it makes us average, a loser, or high class. What matters most with work is doing work that makes you feel good or working for reasons that make you feel good. Fred, a school janitor and a wise man, told me, "I love what I do not because of the work but because it lets me provide for my family. I would do anything to put a roof over our heads and food on the table." Providing for his family is Fred's passion and purpose. That is gratifying for him. He set an example for me and maybe for you too. The lesson I take from Fred is all about the quality of heart and love you put into whatever you do that makes you average or a standout.

LIES Live from Generation to Generation

Rena's father's true passion was art. Recognized as a creative genius by his teachers, George sold insurance to provide for his family. His parents and other well-meaning people told him that was what he *should* do. According to *them*, "No artist ever made a living while he was alive. Most artists starved to death."

George sucked it up, swallowed his passion and potential, and assumed a false identity. He built a successful insurance business and suppressed his love. He denied his calling.

From the earliest time she could remember, to the time of his early death, Rena said her father suffered from depression. "He made a living, but not a life…not one that satisfied or fulfilled him. He had money, but no lasting joy."

Despite his years of silent suffering, when it was time for his beloved daughter to choose a college major, he dissuaded her from pursuing her passion. She too had a gift for artistic expression. At the moment of decision, George passed on to his precious daughter the LIES he was told. "You can't make a living as an artist. You'll starve to death."

A good daughter, afraid of disapproval, the threat of certain failure, and withdrawal of support, she betrayed her own heart. That was more than thirty years ago. Today, feeling trapped and afraid to take the risk of making changes in her life, she lives with regular regret, wishing she had chosen differently back then. She never acknowledges that she has the opportunity to choose again, right now.

Like her father, Rena suffers from depression. Call it a chemical imbalance. It is. But, is the chemical imbalance the cause or a symptom of the real cause, which didn't begin in the brain? It's interesting how seldom we acknowledge the full impact of the compromises we make. There is a high price to pay when we betray ourselves. We concede more than giving up the use of our gifts and talents. We set in motion challenges to our physical and emotional health and well-being.

LIES live, from generation to generation, despite their pain and paralyzing impact.

LIES Live in Organizations Too

Individuals are not the only ones captured by the sabotaging power of false and untested assumptions. Organizations are fertile ground for the breeding and nurturing of *LIES That Limit*. Frequently, I hear people say, "You *can't* take *that* risk. Not here." Or, "The leadership of this company won't tolerate *that*." Or, "I *can't* say *that* to her. The last person who did was (fired, yelled at, demoted, etc.)."

When I hear people make statements like these, I feel compelled to uncover the *LIES* at play. Usually, the LIES – all fear based – are connected to a story, totally or partially factual, about what happened to a person who said or did something similar to the thing that, now, everyone is afraid to do or say.

Hearing assumptions, whenever I can, I probe further. "When did that happen?" People usually wrinkle their brows and look to one another. Finally, a shoulder will shrug and its owner will say, "Gee, I don't know; maybe four or five years ago." Then, to defend their position, the person or a colleague will add, "But, *they* haven't changed. *Nothing* has changed around here."

I marvel at how tightly we hold on to stories that reinforce fear and lead to confinement. We'll take familiar boxes over new and expansive options. We'll settle for what we don't like over having what we want. This enduring saga exists in the workplace, as it does in our private lives.

Journal Your Truth

Which of your dreams have others discounted?

*Which of your dreams have **you** discounted?*

What do you value above your Spirit and Purpose? To what do you give the bulk of your time and energy?

What are the generational LIES in your life — the stories that limit you and others in your family?

Which are you doing more of:
- *Working to make a contribution?*
- *Working primarily to make money?*

Are you a wage slave?

Have you made money your god?

What does your choice — working for money or your mission — contribute to your life?

What does your choice cost you?

Have you found a way to do both — make a contribution aligned with your gifts <u>and</u> make a living? If so, tell us your story. Write to us at info@liesthatlimit.com.

What are the most detrimental LIES exerting controlling influence over your workplace? Over other organizations — for profit and not for profit — you work with and support?

Chapter Seven

LIES Are Liabilities

ᙁᙂ

Limiting LIES Affect Everyone – Even Successful, Savvy You

Adam's story about not being equal to his white peers makes an important point. LIES affect everyone, even the very successful. Even though he had achieved a great deal, he was still suffering from an untruth that he never confronted.

Few, if any of us, are free of *LIES That Limit*. These negative, destructive, minimizing messages are lodged in your belief system, creating unnecessary baggage, weighing you down, and blinding you to the reality of your genius. They hide in the cracks and crevices of your thoughts and behavior patterns, derailing your intention to be your best and fulfill your potential. Unaware of their presence and power, you willfully govern your life according to their edicts.

Limiting LIES are beliefs and ways of operating that may have once served us well. But, today, they're no longer relevant. In fact, they're in the way of our evolution and expression of our full, vital Selves.

Unintentional or intentional LIES; big LIES or little LIES; white LIES or bold-faced LIES; shading, stretching, or spinning the truth – no matter what you call it, the impact is the same. *Distortions mislead, pulling you away from your ability to live and lead your life with a Spirit of Purpose – to be who you were born to be.*

As we look into the LIES in our lives, we may find we're shadow boxing – imagining an opponent that isn't there. There is no one to resist or fight against; no one except the rule-keeper, storyteller, illusionist, and name caller that lives in your mind – also known as *The Border Patrol*. To break free of its tyranny and end the trend of discounting your passion and Purpose, *The Border Patrol* can be and must be challenged, and challenged again.

LIES Create Confusion

When you shackle yourself with fearful thoughts – which are the origin of the *LIES That Limit* – you begin to feel unclear and uncertain. The *shoulds* and *what ifs* pop up. In the presence of the forceful energy of *shoulds* and the unpredictability of *what ifs*, you scare yourself into confusion. Confusion leads to inaction. Feeling unsure and insecure, you become stuck, frozen in the pattern of what has been. Your brain *and* body become paralyzed; your energy stops moving. Nothing is happening – nothing healthy and constructive, that is.

You and I know we're responsible and accountable for the content and quality of our lives. Yet, in subtle ways, and sometimes at readily apparent levels, too many "*I ams, you haves, we don'ts, people like you, people like us, they can'ts, don'ts, shoulds, nevers*" and stories about "*reality*" rule decision-making and govern our lives. They set up barricades you won't walk around, lines you won't cross, territory into which you won't venture, boundaries you won't violate. At those times, you confine yourself to being exactly what you are not – small and innocuous.

If you've heard "*shoulds, what ifs, cant's, nevers, etc.*" or if you say them to yourself, you have been touched by the limiting power of LIES – the Labels, Illusions, Excuses, and Stories we carry concerning what we trust is true and believe is possible. The stuff we call *reality* is usually mental blocks created by our fears, inexperience, or the lack of deep-down determination – a lack of passionate commitment. Passionate commitment overcomes fear, inertia, and inexperience.

LIES Exert Control

Designed to control what you think and do, LIES box you in, imprisoning you in a life of silent suffering. They define what's "right" and prescribe the range of choices you believe are available. LIES become the standard by which you judge yourself and others.

LIES dominate your thinking and exert undue, undeserved control over too much of life. Ruling your thoughts and beliefs, restrictive Labels, Illusions, Excuses, and Stories define what you see and believe is possible and appropriate. It matters not that LIES are false conceptions.

Borne out of historical traditions and cultural customs — familial and societal — LIES are passed on as THE truth. You respond accordingly. Believing them, living your life based on them, you empower LIES and disempower your Self. You choose against your Self in favor of living up to the demands of LIES.

Limiting Labels, Illusions, Excuses, and Stories have a detrimental effect. They distort your thinking, causing you to lose clarity about what *you* want and need. Muddled thinking diminishes self-confidence. Short on confidence, faith, and trust, your ability to take care of yourself falters and you feel compelled to search for external validation. You look out there, wanting to get it from *them*. Happily, the world obliges and assumes control. You no longer own your Self.

Through the use of obvious and subtle means, the world around you exerts control over your life. Pressures to conform, fit in, and gain the approval of others, result in a loss. Free will — your right to choose for yourself and craft your own course — is dialed down, deactivated, disengaged. In its place, the need for approval and acceptance reigns. *Their* judgment carries more weight than the value you place on being true to the call of your Spirit and Purpose — the energy you were born to express, the path you were born to walk. In so doing, you give up the truth of who you really are in exchange for avoiding the pain you perceive will come as a result of *their* disapproval.

LIES Cover Worthiness

Much of the fear and resistance to what we say we want is caused by a deeper issue, one that is hard to detect and few of us would admit to. It's the matter of worthiness. It's embedded in the foundation of our thinking. Beneath shying away from visibility, not fully utilizing our talents, or resisting going against the grain to pursue our calling, lay questions like:

Am I good enough to...?

Am I worthy of...?

Do I know enough to...?

Am I smart enough to...?

Why do I deserve...when so many others don't have...?

These questions of worthiness and enough-ness exist because we are not our real Selves.

So, the answer is NO; we are not enough when we live in the shadow of our Spirit. We can only be enough and feel worthy when we live from our core, aligned with our Spirit and Purpose. When your real Self is present, then and only then will you feel so full the question of enough will not even occur to you.

LIES Are De-energizing

Whenever I feel exhausted or de-energized, I know LIES have a hold on me. When I'm overwhelmed, frustrated, or feel like blaming others for what I'm experiencing – too much to do, too many deadlines, too many people depending on me, I know LIES are at the root of it all. If I'm ill at ease or feel cheated out of joy, peace of mind, and the freedom to be who I was born to be, I know that Labels, Illusions, Excuses, and Stories – erroneous beliefs and habits of mind – are at work.

Instead of being in the mode of self-oppression or reacting reflexively at those times, my work is to engage in a process of *intentional reflection,* making *conscious choice* possible. Later, in Chapter Twelve, I'll describe a number of tools and techniques you can use to assess who's in control at any given moment – you or the LIES in your life.

LIES Are Tricky

Labels, Illusions, Excuses, and Stories are tricky. You may feel that because you're not doing what you think *they* want you to do, you're not allowing *them* to control you. When, in fact, they're still in the driver's seat and you're the unwitting passenger. If you're reacting to others, you're still not freely defining your destiny.

Jon was tricked by LIES. Shy and awkward, he really wanted to be accepted. As a youngster, he was nerdy and not athletic — thick glasses, brainy, not a cool dresser or smooth talker. Jon was not hip. He tried to be one of the guys, only to be rejected time and again. Eventually he gave up.

Pretending he didn't need or even want people to like him, he took on the persona of a critical, hot-tempered, indifferent person. This identity was not the real Jon, not deep down. It was a reaction to pain. At his core, he longed for affection and closeness, for relationships. He wanted to belong. In reaction to *them*, he designed a life that didn't fit who he really is. He was a lonely man, hiding behind a mask of indifference. By not being true to himself, he rejected himself. He did to himself what pained him so in relationships with others. Both he and they ultimately rejected him. No one loved him.

Public opinion matters to us — it matters a lot. We long to fit in, even when we have to contort ourselves and force the fit. It diminishes who we are and takes us off track, off purpose. We desert our own special path, sabotaging our prospects for fulfillment. In the end, we feel we've wasted our life force and precious time on earth.

Tricked and trapped by LIES, we risk being emotionally and spiritually bankrupt. Had we chosen to live life as we dreamed — as singer-songwriter Jill Scott says, "Living My Life Like It's Golden" — we wouldn't suffer the hollow pain and disappointment of a joy-less, uninspired, and uninspiring life. The price we pay for ignoring our calling, burying our sense of Purpose is high. Yet, the illusion is just the opposite.

Believing the LIES, we conclude that the cost of following our own hearts and minds is too high. Instead, we take the real risk and cater to the needs and desires of our small-minded, fearful Selves.

When you realize you are a Spirit of Purpose, you will have the courage to walk alone, to chart a new and unique course; not in reaction to anything or anyone, but because it's genuinely what speaks to you and fills you with lasting goodness.

LIES Reduce You to Average Size

His eyes twinkled as he engaged in a little cultural mischief aimed at teaching me, the American, an important bit of Aussie wisdom. "You should never be the tall Poppy," said my Australian client. Predictably, he continued with his explanation. "You know what that means don't you?"

"No," I said.

"Out in the field, the tall poppy is the first to be cut down. So, you don't want to be the tall poppy and stand out. It's too dangerous. You are an easy target."

Wow! That was it in a nutshell. The admonition and threat were worldwide: *be small like the rest of us. Don't stand out or we'll cut you down to size.* The cultural push to be normal and fit in is strong and mostly unconscious. The demand to be like the rest of us is positioned as the right way; making a divergent path, and the person who creates and follows it, is wrong.

Fitting in, being seen as normal, requires denial of authentic self-expression. Fearing you don't have a right to say "No" to them and "Yes!" to your Spirit, you're reduced to something less than who you really are. Deserting your unique identity, you become average, vanilla, inauthentic. *The Border Patrol* now stationed deep inside your mind keeps you in line through implied and overt threats that evoke fear and result in mindless compliance. Eventually you become the self-enforcer of the *LIES That Limit* you. Self-oppressed, you trade your passion for survival. As the force of habit and cultural stories take over, awareness of your deeper Self recedes and fades. Other people and circumstances define you. No longer your own authority, you look outside yourself for meaning and validation.

Journal Your Truth

With what are you shadow boxing — imagining an opponent or barrier that isn't really there?

About what are you feeling unclear or uncertain? Which LIES are at work, clouding your clarity?

Which "shoulds" and "what ifs" are scaring you and holding you back?

About what are you suffering silently? Which LIES are at work in this area of your thought process and life?

Where are you tricked by LIES, allowing them to waste your time and sap your energy?

Chapter Eight

Living LIES

LIES Are Blocks

LIES block access to the truth of who you are and what you're here to do. You begin to feel as if there is no use in trying to find happiness. This is just the way it is. Optimism obliterated, you feel stuck and hopeless. *The Border Patrol*, keeper of the status quo, reminds you, "Things don't change," "There's no chance of the situation being different." Have you noticed how easily feeling stuck morphs into frustration, anger, and depression? Soon you begin to think, "There is no sense in trying."

The Labels, Illusions, Excuses, and Stories have defeated you — they've beaten you down, robbed you of energy and vitality, and diminished your zest for life. The more stuck you feel, the more tangible and real the blocks feel. The boundaries they establish seem firm, fixed, impenetrable, immovable, and unconquerable. Inwardly, you hear, "I guess I'll just have to learn to live with this."

By settling, the very thing you should have charge over — your life — no longer belongs to you. You're trapped in a story that isn't one of your conscious making.

Disempowered, joy and creativity snuffed out, you go on with life. But, it's never the same. Your life becomes something different from, less than, the life you really want. It's not the life you dreamed of or longed for. You barely feel alive at all. Why is that? Maybe it's because you've killed off your connection to your core Self, your Spirit, and your Purpose. You chose limits over life, the false teachings and ideas of others over your own wise inner voice — the voice that prompts you toward your truth, toward the real you.

LIES are beliefs, ideas, concepts, explanations, scripts, and stories that exist in your mind, where all beliefs reside. Every mindset you have is one of the LIES you let in and allowed to take up residence. That being so, with vigilance, you can identify the ones that hold you back, and let them go.

Really, letting go of LIES is as simple as changing your mind. Yet, it doesn't seem so simple; does it? In fact, it can feel like an awesome, overwhelming, nearly impossible task. With determination, you can release yourself from the stranglehold of Labels, Illusions, Excuses, and Stories and release the power of your passion.

LIES Hold You Back

LIES result in a loss of authenticity; you lose track of who you are, and your ability to love – both yourself and others – is diminished. What blocks your happiness and success seems to exist in the outer world. "If only they would treat me with more respect." "If only they would give me a chance." "If only I could find someone who really loves and understands me, then I would be happy."

When you live LIES, happiness and satisfaction are fleeting. The feeling lasts for a while and then fades as soon as the thing or person or situation you thought would make you happy doesn't do the trick anymore. The salve no longer soothes the ache. Ranging from annoying to intense, the pain is back and you find yourself on the hunt for another solution.

Seldom does it occur to us that what we really want and need is a closer relationship with our core essence. You are the answer to whatever ails you. In fact, you are your only problem and you, the real you, are the only solution that will satisfy your longing.

LIES are blocks and barriers that hold you back and keep you down. You allow them to deny you your greatness, your genius. LIES do not allow you to make full use of your gifts and talents, nor to fulfill your purpose. LIES deny you a passionate and sane life.

Awesome becomes average when you choose to succumb to the *shoulds* and *can'ts* that roam about your mind. Awesome remains average for as long as you permit *The Border Patrol* to define and bind your life.

LIES Waste Time — *Tick-Talk, Tick-Talk*

Time and your life keep moving, and you may do what many talented people do – you pretend talking about your grand vision is the same as living it. This is what the average person does. It's the "I want to…, but …". I know this pattern well. I was seduced by what I call *Tick-Talk, Tick-Talk* until a close friend called me to task. *Tick-Talk, Tick-Talk* describes what happens when all you're doing is talking; time is passing while you're talking and not acting.

"Are you ever going to do anything besides write down your ideas and talk about what you'll do when?" asked my friend.

Ouch! And, Thank God! That jab sparked action. I took concerted action to make what I had been dreaming about happen. That confrontation about all talk and no action served me well. I had to look at myself and ask, "Why am I not taking action to start my own business?" The answer was easy – fear. I was afraid to leave the comforts and my fantasy of the security I had in my corporate job. I mean what if…? What if I can't do it? What if I can't attract clients? What if they won't award me with contracts? What if I can't replace my salary? What if I fail and can't find another job? On and on my list of fears went.

At first, I listened to my fears rumble around in my head; my neck and shoulders tense, my gut tight and churning. Then I wrote my *what ifs* down and wrote out "answers" next to each one. That's a technique I use to address the terror *The Border Patrol* likes to stir.

Then I created a plan – a road map for how I would make it happen and what I needed financially to feel safe proceeding. I prepared a year's worth of income – my net, not gross income – that would give me a good foundation. I made two additional agreements with myself. First, I would work at getting a contract to provide service to my current employer. Second, I would give myself a full year of all out effort to make it work. If I had no paid work twelve months after quitting, I would look for another corporate job. Again, another strategy for soothing the fear of failure that *The Border Patrol* wanted me to give in to. Remember it likes the status quo – that's its job, keeper of current conditions.

The plan worked. That was 1987, and here I am today, enjoying the thrills and challenges of evolving, growing, and running my own business.

Had I not been called out, I might never have tried my hand at making my dream a reality.

The same is true about writing this book. *Tick-Talk, Tick-Talk* played a role here too. Some of it was valid, learning how to write, incubating ideas, clarifying my thinking, choosing to give attention to important family matters, running my business, etc. And some of it was procrastination, staving off what I feared would be inevitable failure and embarrassment about my inability to produce a valuable and successful book.

At no time was my fear as clear as I've stated it. Usually my delays could be logically explained. That's the cover, the smoke screen put up by *The Border Patrol* – the keeper of LIES and the barriers to personal freedom and expression they set up.

Watch Out for *The Border Patrol*

Watch out for the seductively corrective voice of *The Border Patrol* – the one who keeps you in line by injecting fear-filled LIES that sound as if they're helpful and protective. In actuality, the LIES keep you focused on the world outside of you as a dangerous, hazardous place. *The Border Patrol* doesn't want you to notice the self-imposed LIES and limits inherent in statements such as:

"You know you can't do that."

"No one has ever done that before."

"Wait a minute. Do you know what you're getting into?"

"That's for other people, not you."

"Wait! The time isn't right. First, you need to..."

"Oh, my God. My daughter is a lesbian. She'll never have a normal life (I've failed as a parent. I won't have grandchildren.)."

"You're too old."

"You were never...anyway. Why do you think you can...now?"

"Women don't..."

"Men don't..."

"You're not smart enough to…"

"You didn't go to the right school for…"

"My…[insert the name of the applicable person] won't understand."

"I can't be honest with…, I don't want to hurt her/him/them."

If you take an objective look at the pointless, ridiculous, life-defying restrictions you allow to guide your decisions and actions, you'll probably laugh. And you know the limits that restrictions establish are not funny. They are the source of endless, drip-drip-drip pain and suffering.

Instead of focusing on fears, put attention on finding ways to be free of the messages in your mind that don't serve you and allow you to be your full, best Self. For the woman who worried that her daughter is lesbian, instead of worrying about who her daughter makes love with, she could be glad for her daughter's ability to love and experience sensual and sexual pleasure.

The Influence of Erroneous Assumptions

As discussed earlier, when you look at the lives of others — individuals, families, cultural groups, societies — you can easily identify many of the beliefs they carry that don't support their best interests. You can name the beliefs that are problematic and interfere with their effectiveness; beliefs that aren't true, they just treat them as if they are. They use the false beliefs to make decisions about how to live their lives, lead other people, manage their family, govern the community.

The influence of erroneous assumptions is clear and pervasive. It becomes most obvious when we look back in history — the history of our family, our cultural groups, the society in which we grew up and the broader world in which we live. The evidence is clear to us. People believe LIES. LIES are at the foundation of a good part of our lives.

But, the *LIES That Limit* YOU, well, that's another story. These LIES — Labels, Illusions, Excuses, and Stories — are much harder to see. Mostly, we experience their negative and limiting effects and wonder, "Why in the world are things not going my way? Why do I not feel fulfilled when I have every *thing* I've always wanted? Why am I'm struggling so much, every day?

Why am I not at peace? Why can't I find my way out of this situation and into a better one?"

It's because you believe the LIES in your life. You hold them as reality, not the pliable, even false, concepts they are.

This book is designed to encourage you to embark on a journey of self-discovery, really. Uncovering the truth of who you really are. Not who others say you are or *should* be, but who you – at your core, in your Spirit, your heart of hearts – feel and know you are.

Become more self-aware. That is, more aware of the real you. The you that may have been denied, pushed down, forgotten, undernourished, or ignored, as you struggled to survive in your family, relationships, workplace, and community.

What everyone else is doing may not be right for you. In fact, LIES live on the energy of, "Everyone does it this way. Therefore, it must be right." You are unique. What you want may align with what some others do, or maybe not. You have to find your way, make your own decision in order to craft a life that is yours. Not your mother's or father's; not that teacher or guidance counselor who told you what you would never become; not your religion's idea of what is right for you. No! I want to encourage you to find the truth within your Self. That is what will enable you to feel seen and loved, to be happy, healthy, successful, and satisfied.

Get beyond the rules that deny truth and keep you stuck and limited. Let go of all that keeps us from respecting and loving ourselves enough to be true to who we really are, to be true to our calling, passion, and sense of Purpose. When the real you is known and expressed, you will finally be at peace.

Letting go of the *LIES That Limit* YOU is all that you have to do to be free of the blocks in your life. It's all in how you think about the stuff of your life, how you conceive of it, and how you define yourself, as a result.

Journal Your Truth

In what ways do you live by other people's policies?

What greatness is in you that you have yet to express?

What have you been talked out of doing?

What contribution do you feel called and compelled to make to your:
- *Family?*
- *Community?*
- *Workplace?*
- *The world?*

What do you do when your exciting idea is met with, "It's a good idea, but it won't work"? Or, "You can't do that. No one here has ever done that."

Is Tick-Talk, Tick-Talk part of your reality? How so?

What is the critical voice in your head — The Border Patrol — saying to stifle your willingness to act?

Chapter Nine

LIES in My Life

☯

Uncovering the LIES in My Life

Though not always welcomed guests in conversations with others – especially to those wedded to tradition – to one degree or another, I've thought about and questioned the assumptions I make, the stories I faithfully repeat, and the rules I've revered for as long as I can remember. Questions like, "Is that really *true?* Why do I have to do it *that* way? Who says? How can you be so sure? What makes *them* right?" have always been with me.

Traditionalists count on the coercive power of corrective conversation. Chastisement and criticism are used to keep you in line. I had such a discussion when I was about twenty-two.

A close friend said to me, "You don't think the rules apply to you, do you?" It wasn't really a question, or a compliment. The energy that came from him was full of rage, scorn, and accusation. I wasn't playing by *his* rules. He wanted power over me, and I would have none of that.

It's funny, I was afraid of his big, blustery, critical energy. At the same time, I felt fear rise up in my gut – that's *The Border Patrol* at work. I thought to myself, "This is ridiculous. He must be crazy." Looking him in the eye, trembling, I took a deep breath and replied, "No, I don't. The rules apply to anyone who believes them. I don't believe them."

I think it was my higher Self, my Spirit, speaking that day, encouraging and educating me. I'll never forget that moment. It was potent and established a new emotional root, one that would help me honor my Self. Until that moment of truth, how I felt about LIES, limits, and coercion hadn't been so clear. I hadn't grasped the depth of my commitment to finding my own way and thoughtfully determining the rules I live by. An important eye-opener, that interaction helped me realize I have to remain vigilant and not allow what others think or do to be the defining influence in my life. Needless to say, it is an ongoing task, a lifelong commitment.

A World of Stark Contrasts

Maybe it was my proximity to the roots of slavery in the United States, or a past-life memory, or my disdain for the nonsensical edicts offered by the world around me, but something in me wanted to be free. Born in rule-bound, rural South Carolina, we lived in a three-room wooden shack owned by the family on whose land we lived. Previously inhabited by slaves, there was no sheetrock, plaster, or paneling to create walls. Studs with boards nailed to one side, made up room dividers and the external walls. We had no running water or indoor plumbing, just a pump in the yard and bushes and trees for privacy.

My parents worked as day laborers in the fields, planting and harvesting crops, picking cotton, hoeing peanuts and soybeans, suckling and stringing tobacco. My maternal grandmother, who lived with us, worked in the house of the landowner. On days when Mrs. Edlyn didn't need her "at the house," she too worked in the fields. My brother and I, from the time we were small, also did farm work.

This was a time and place of stark contrasts. The differences in the lives of the races were palpable. The distinction between the haves and have-nots was striking, regardless of race. This was not a place or time of great hope or opportunity, especially for an impoverished, young black child, not if you looked at it *objectively* and faced *reality*. This was a time and place where belief in hard work, struggle, sacrifice, and service to a God, whose wrath we feared, prevailed. It was hard to do more than live day to day, hand to mouth. Aspirations were low and considered ill advised. Why want, when you can't have? You only disappoint yourself in the end.

It's hard to let go of where you begin. The lessons live in your bones. They become part of your DNA. They are the soup in which you sit. Like a strong marinade, those lessons infuse your every thought, feeling, and action. What you hear others say, what you see them do and experience, shapes your view of life, which defines what you trust to be true. That is, until you begin to question those beliefs and expand your experiences.

Even in that place of clear, harsh contrasts and apparently limited options, I wondered, "Why not me? I don't want *this*; I want *that*. Why can't *I* do what *I* want to?" I would think to myself, "If that person can do it, so can I." At bolder moments, I would quietly think, because I dared not speak it, "Just because *you* can't doesn't mean *I* can't."

Back then I didn't know where these ideas came from. Today, I know they came from deep inside – from the wiser, timeless, know-no-boundaries part of me. That part of me caused me to challenge what I witnessed. This is my Spirit, my core – the wise and wonderful power that is each of us. Spirit speaks in this way – through feelings, ideas, and promptings – helping you to see and know the boundaries that you are perceiving are not the limits of possibilities.

Spirit is energy, an invisible guiding force that supplies life-saving thoughts, inspiring feelings, positive direction, and courage. Spirit helps us see a wider range of positive possibilities even when the view is obscured and bleak. Spirit says, "Look over here. There is another way, a better way, should *you choose* to pursue it."

Spirit, or core essence, shows you a way that is uniquely yours. *If* you don't allow others to talk you out of following the direction your soul's guidance provides, *if* you don't allow the conditions your eyes behold to be the only limits of reality you trust and place your faith in, Spirit will expand your awareness and your world.

More and more, I listen to and follow the leads of Spirit. Sometimes the direction I receive defies logic. More often than not, the direction is contrary to false wisdom provided by the Labels, Illusions, Excuses, and Stories – the LIES – I've been conditioned to believe. Spirit has led me to a more expansive life, one of greater personal freedom and a willingness to be responsible and accountable for what I experience and create.

An Early Look at LIES

On a particularly beautiful spring day, when I was twenty-seven, I sat at an outdoor café with a friend, basking in the noonday sun, watching the center-city Philadelphia lunch crowd. It was a moment like many my friend and I shared; nothing extraordinary, just girlfriends enjoying laughs over lunch. That is, until *they* walked by. In that moment, an ordinary day became a day that has had a lasting impact.

They were three white men; twenty-something young "turks," clad in long-sleeved blue dress shirts, tucked in of course, complemented by conservative ties and belted, khaki dress pants; the quintessential preppies, up-and-coming executives, behaving as if they owned the world.

Donna spoke first. "Look at those three white boys; just as arrogant as they wanna be. They _all_ think they own the world."

I added ruefully, "They probably will own it someday. Someone will give it to them, just because they showed up. That's the way it works."

We laughed – kind of – in the way one does when the matter isn't really funny. It was the type of laughter that covers deeper feelings; feelings laced with a long legacy of anger, hurt, and a good measure of envy.

Something shifted that day. While voicing my judgments, a startling insight occurred to me. I blurted out, "Those white boys are free. Nothing's holding them back. They're not thinking about what they *can't* do. They think they have the right and ability to do anything they want. *Why don't I?*"

A new awareness dawned in me. I realized I was keeping racism alive in my mind every time I doubted my right and ability to pursue my dreams.

My young eyes opened to new a reality, a fresh possibility, *what if I have been limiting myself based on LIES?* What if the, "No, *you* can'ts…" in my life, the ones that felt solid, objective, and bought in to – like real, tangible barriers – were more related to what I had been taught? What if that was truth and I lived based on *that* idea instead of the cultural stories that restricted access to what I wanted, resulting in fearful feelings, even hopelessness about trying or having high expectations?

That day, I decided I would no longer dash my hopes, lower my expectations, or set up false boundaries. I promised myself I would challenge every "*You* can't," "*They* won't let *you*," "*That* will never happen," and stop accepting self-imposed "restraining orders" as fact. Little did I know that freeing myself from limiting LIES would become a lifelong process, and my message to the world.

Today, I wish I could find those three young men to thank them. They mirrored another way; a way that was available to me, if I chose it. They modeled the freedom I always desired and didn't know was within my power to possess — not until that day.

Friend to friend, I spoke my life-changing affirmation to Donna. "I'm going to stop discouraging myself, minimizing who I am, and what I have a right to."

Donna smiled and said simply, "Alright now!"

The Good Stuff Comes *After* Life?

I believe our lives have meaning. We exist on earth, at this time, for a reason. Everyone is significant and has a role to play in making the world — no matter the size of your world — a better place. These beliefs have been a part of my reality, for as long as I can remember.

Growing up, as I watched people around me, it seemed few felt their lives were a meaningful, grand experience. Burdened by the drudgery and weight of day-to-day existence, most seemed guided by the belief that the best part of life would come when they died. They talked about "going to a better place," or "laying down my burdens," all after the end of life in the body.

Yet, no one looked forward to or hurried to meet death, at least not consciously or admittedly. In fact, the majority appeared to do all they could to prolong physical life. Few, if any, had real joy or satisfaction, at least not in any sustained way.

I thought it strange to believe I was born to live on earth with the sole purpose of waiting for death so life could then be good and have meaning. Something was wrong with that idea. It seemed unloving, an unfair waste. Something of critical importance was missing; it had to be.

Over time, I concluded I had been taught LIES. The missing element was created by the illusion that the good stuff came after this life ended. If you survived the trials and tribulations of your time here on earth and lived by a strict code of conduct, then you would earn passage through the Pearly Gates — Voila! There you were; you were "in," home free, walking the streets of gold and listening to the majestic choir sing all day, every day.

While beautiful and consistent with the Christian beliefs I had been taught, that notion made no sense to me. There had to be a reason why we were here; one that made my physical life and the present significant. I decided two things. First, the proposition that the only reason I'm here is to prepare for death and heaven was a false belief, though spoken as if it were true. Second, I would not shape my life based on that notion. I chose to focus on the life-giving, here and now, dimension of God.

I wanted to live as if every day was important and, even more so, as if there was a reason for my presence on earth. I wanted to live as if the God talked about in church was my friend and ally, not my judge and punisher. I wanted to be connected to God, here and now, on earth, in the way the preacher and my elders promised I would be once I died and went to heaven, provided I behaved appropriately.

My Friend and Guide

I began to talk with God, my friend and guide. Important illusions were dispelled. I became aware of God as *both* Him and Her, masculine and feminine. I was blown away when I realized God was not a person or personality, like I had been taught. I came to understand God is energy – all-knowing, all-powerful, all-creative, all-loving energy. Energy that makes the invisible visible. Energy that creates worlds. Energy that manifests through each person – through me and everyone I know, even those with whom I disagreed, didn't like how they chose to live and behave, or didn't understand their traditions and worldview.

My awareness expanded through my growing relationship with this amazing energy. It became clear that everyone has equal value. That was different from what I had been taught, and what I saw play out in my community and the world. There, the prevailing illusion was that some people – individuals and cultural groups – were better, more important, and more valuable than others. The most worthy had a right, a responsibility even, to dictate how the world works.

I wanted neither to tell others what they must do, think, and feel, nor to be told. Given my drive to be free, I could only believe others wanted the same. *That* just seemed right and respectful.

Occasionally, people around me would talk about their special talents and skills, what they enjoyed doing or always wanted to try. The person's unspoken message usually contained a quality of, "It sure would be nice *if...but,* that's not possible." Or, "It's not *realistic* for me to..." Ultimately, the person would vocalize his conclusion, "Well, no use crying over spilled milk." Or, "That's water under the bridge. I guess I'd better leave that idea alone before I upset myself." Or, "No use thinking about that now. I guess it just wasn't the Lord's will."

Why Blame God?

When at a loss for words to convey my thoughts and feelings, or lacking understanding about why I was having certain experiences, I too have said, "I guess it wasn't the Lord's will." It's an easy statement to make, one that allows you to not examine your choices and actions, or be accountable for what happens in your life. In truth, I often saw those same people who said, "It wasn't the Lord's will," making decisions that curtailed the pursuit of their dreams. Giving up working on their own behalf, they turned around and blamed God for their condition. It struck me as both ridiculous and irresponsible to think that way. Of course, I never said as much, not until now.

Back then I didn't want to face the fierce correction I felt my way of seeing God and life would elicit. Today, I feel differently. Now, I'm willing to share my beliefs.

Search for Happiness and Meaning (We Want the Same Thing)

Do you want to be happy and certain that your life, day to day, matters and has meaning? I do. Judging from what I've heard others say, most people do. In so many ways, we all want the same thing. Our way of getting to it may be different and yield a wide range of results, but the goal is the same. We want to know we matter, our lives have meaning, and we make a difference — all of which leads to happiness.

I've searched for happiness in the usual ways, looking in all the usual places — I've looked for it in professional achievement; in good girl, nice person behavior; in volunteerism; and in church involvement and dedication to a religious path.

I've looked in relationships and finding the "right" one. I really thought I could find "the right one." I didn't know *I* had to *be* in the right relationship with my Self before I could have a healthy relationship with another person.

I looked in independence from relationships – you know the "I don't need anybody else to be happy" pretense. While that statement is true, at that point in my evolution, it was a defensive stance in the face of my failure in relationships. It didn't reflect the high truth of, "I am whole and complete, and not dependent on anyone else to make me happy." I now know we bring our full Selves into relationships, not just wounded fragments looking to be made whole.

The quest for happiness and meaning drives all of us. Advertisers certainly know this. They prey on our vulnerability and desperation to find "the answer" – the cure to our emptiness created by the absence of internal joy and meaning. They offer us antidotes that profit others and cost not just dollars, but real lasting joy. They tell us to buy "stuff," promising it will make us happy and fulfilled. They say the right stuff – their specific stuff – will close the gaping hole and satisfy our need.

I bought that idea. Did you?

Lacking many basic necessities and all creature comforts, growing up poor I was sure that as soon as I could supply those needs, I would have it made. Poverty and lack, an early *Pivot Point*, contributed to my erroneous belief that happiness could be bought; that stuff created fulfillment and security. After all, that was the cultural story, and it was confirmed by the way I interpreted what I saw around me.

In my community and everywhere I looked, people with resources seemed to smile more; though they didn't laugh as much. Their lives seemed easy and nice. They lived in beautiful, immaculate homes. They had cars that didn't break down; and they seemed to treat each other politely, tenderly. Seemingly without worry, they had food to eat, money to spend, nice clothes to wear, good schools to attend, fun friends, and exciting activities. They took vacations that didn't involve a car ride to visit family. The images of material success were all around me. I bought the meaning I attributed to the images and unknowingly birthed LIES.

With pretty pictures in mind, I set out to make my world nice. It was fun to set a goal and achieve it. To buy my first house, my first car, my first business suit, my first piece of good jewelry, to take my family on a real vacation – not only to visit relatives. One nice thing led to another. Then, literally, the desire for nice things grew and grew. I felt insatiable, like an over-eater, alcoholic, or drug addict. Soon, I learned that stuff led to a hunger and thirst for more stuff. Something important was obviously missing; I could feel it.

Years of accumulation and I was surrounded and suffocating, I began to choke. The acquisition and management of stuff consumes a lot of life! My stuff forced the real me, who I wasn't yet acquainted with but could feel the absence of, out to the far edges of my life. Spirit had to sit and wait. I could *feel* the empty space, but wasn't quite sure what caused it or what it was about. The way I knew to address it was to get more and do more. I became a member of the AA Club – Achieve and Acquire.

Stuff became central, requiring physical and emotional energy, time, and attention – lots of care and feeding. Emotionally I felt nauseated by the sheer volume of it, and burdened by the work involved in acquiring and maintaining it. I began divorcing myself from it, shedding it. Clearly, stuff did not make me happy or give my life meaning. I had to lighten my load, I felt an internal tug, a longing, and noticed that something important was missing. What was it?

The missing element was close at hand, but I was too busy to notice its quiet presence. I only felt its absence. The idea that a satisfying solution was as close as connecting to my inner world – my Spirit – hadn't occurred to me.

She Can, But *She* Can't

Every fall, without fail, my husband, Bill, and I go to St. John, in the U.S. Virgin Islands. One evening, we took the ferry over to St. Thomas and had dinner at the Wikked Café. Sitting on the covered porch, enjoying the tropical breeze and watching the sun set over Yacht Haven Marina, our waitress introduced herself.

"Hi. I'm Melanie. What can I get you to drink...Rum Punch...a Hurricane...maybe a Mango Margarita?"

I liked her instantly. She had a warm, bright smile and interacted with ease. She seemed pleased with herself; satisfied deep down.

During the course of the evening we chatted, sharing stories. She was from Minnesota; graduated high school and came to St. Thomas to work for the season. That was nearly two years ago. She never left.

"I love it here. I work two jobs — one as a waitress, here, and the other on a day boat that takes people out snorkeling and diving. I'm happy, I love it here."

As she walked away, I said to Bill, "I admire that young woman. That could be Aja," his daughter, my stepdaughter.

He retorted, "Did you notice? That young lady is white. She can spin this experience into a tale of how she took time off to find her self and worked her way up from server to restaurant manager. Aja wouldn't stand a chance if she did that. People would call her a lazy bum."

He laughed. I smiled at him, not in agreement, but because I love him. The cumulative effect of cultural conditioning was speaking. As the words left his mouth, I could tell he was feeling a little uncomfortable. He quickly added, "Or maybe that's one of the LIES."

I was proud. He caught himself telling a tale of limitation. "Yes. You're right, it's one of many LIES we live. How will we ever know what we can do, unless we try?"

Race aside, for most people, many things we believe and say as if they're fact, we don't actually like or want to claim as our reality. Yet, seldom do we test the truism. We simply allow it to roll off our tongue, repeating old messages, keeping the same stories alive, imprisoning and holding ourselves down. We're lost in LIES of limitation.

Perhaps what Bill said was more accurate for earlier generations. Back then, not enough of us investigated our assumptions by pushing the boundaries we believed were there. We didn't venture outside the dominant thinking of the time to see if another set of possibilities existed. Feeling stuck, we lived the LIES we were told defined our lot, for the sake of survival.

"Get an education. Find a good job. Work hard. Keep your nose clean. Stay with that company until you retire. We didn't even think about careers, let alone an adventure in the Caribbean," I added.

No sooner did the words leave my mouth than I caught myself.

"Oh my, LIES are flying out of my mouth, too. I know blacks who, generations ago, defied the restrictions of social convention. They created their own lives, pursued their dreams and calling." I thought of Harriet Tubman, conductor of The Underground Railroad. Then, together, we named people we know personally who didn't allow themselves to be reduced to average size; who didn't shrink from the call to be more. We knew people, black people, who didn't accept the ruling assumptions of the day. "*You* can't do *that*" didn't stop them from blazing their own trail.

Risk aside, some people have given themselves freedom to craft their lives as they wanted. So what caused the two of us – two reasonable, smart, and successful people – to say the opposite, to repeat a story of restriction? It's simple. We didn't pause to think.

Instead of agreeing with and repeating the messages of the past, what if you paused and took time to think *before* you say those well-worn words or use that familiar expression that keeps a specific way of thinking and behaving alive? How might you confront the LIES in your life with that simple act? Catch yourself in a cliché, and ask if it is truth.

Journal Your Truth

Which truisms do you want to test?

What are your unasked questions and challenges to traditional assumptions?

Which of your "tangible barriers" are LIES?

With whom do you engage in coercive, corrective conversation? What do you imagine the impact to be on their Spirit of Purpose?

What is your quest for meaning and happiness driving you toward?

What positive possibility is Spirit showing you?

How can you make a conscious choice to look and listen, and follow the leading Spirit provides?

Chapter Ten

Beginning to See Differently

What Happens Along the Way?

In the beginning and toward the end, we are clearest. We know who we are; what we want; and what's important.

Along the way, what happens to our awareness of who we really are? What happens to the truth we knew so well, early on, and rediscover years later? How is it that we turn away from our Self and toward something or someone else?

What *They* Think

Due to illnesses that have diminished her capacity to fully care for herself, my mother's home is an assisted living facility. There are about a hundred other people in her community who range in age from early 60s to 100 plus.

These days Mom spends time reviewing her life; looking back over her past, assessing, re-enjoying the pleasurable, and making peace with the painful. She and her neighbor-friends share such conversations. Every once in a while, she lets my brother, Lee, and me in on her thoughts.

Lee told me of a gem Mom shared with him. She said, "I really regret how much attention I paid to what other people thought and said."

Mom, like a lot of us, acted in reaction to what others *might* think or say. Enslaved to public opinion, often without ever knowing what *they* really think, we live LIES we've made up. We treat them as if they're truth; they become the basis for our actions and reactions. Losing connection to our own truth, to what really matters to us, we are no longer free to be our Selves – the unique beings we were born to be.

Imagining what *they* think or say, we become tense, afraid, imprisoned by negative fantasies rampaging our minds, disturbing our peace. All the while, *they* are probably not thinking about us. And, if they are, so what?!

Misdirecting the focus of our attention, we suffer the consequences until we consciously decide to take back control, reclaiming power over our own lives.

Where Have You Abdicated Authority?

For too many of us, too much of the time, we're vulnerable to public scrutiny and criticism. When *they* praise us, we feel good. Feelings of devastation develop when *they* disapprove. Public opinion pulls us toward them, closer to what *they* think. Others of us use *their* views as our launching pad, propelling ourselves in the opposite direction, pretending we don't care what *they* say. But, all the while, we're actually moving in reaction to *them* and *their* perspective. With that reaction, they still have a hold on us.

I'll use myself as an example. An empathetic person, I'm acutely attuned to energy and emotion – the invisible stuff of life – the stuff you feel more than see. I often know what others are feeling before they recognize it themselves. When people love me, I know it and feel it intensely. When people dislike me, I feel that intensely too. One of the last things I want is the pain of criticism and rejection. Writing a book about a topic like this, I feel exposed as I put my views and life experiences out in the open. As a result, it's taken me nearly fifteen years to step up to this calling. I didn't want to face my worst fears – criticism and rejection. I didn't want to stand out and risk being called out. That's my fear of public scrutiny.

I've used this fear to ignore the direction I felt called to follow; even when the direction seemed clear and compelling, I disregarded the guidance of Spirit. I chose not to look and sound different and articulate the depth of my point of view. Too often, I stand in that middle place, that no-man's land. Truth doesn't live there. While I may appear to fit in and not offend, I'm inauthentic and lifeless. What's more, I've scrutinized and rejected my Self.

There is no worse fate than self-denial, self-sabotage, and self-abandonment. Who can you trust when you can't trust yourself to stand up for yourself? The answer: Spirit. You can always trust Spirit. Spirit stands by waiting for the moment you're ready to embrace who you really are and to stand in your truth. For me, on this matter, the moment is now.

Who Makes You Happy?

I usually visit Mom a couple of times a week. Waiting for the elevator, or walking down the halls, I have an opportunity to interact with her neighbors, as well as the staff. One of my favorites is Joanie, Mom's good friend since she moved to her new "neighborhood."

Mom and Joanie enjoy meals together, and attend activities and social events. Daily, each checks on the other. They're good girlfriends.

As I approached the elevator in the lobby one morning, Joanie was sitting in her favorite spot right near the elevator door. I greeted her as usual, "Hi Joanie. How are you today?"

"I'm fine, honey. "

"Are you giving yourself a good day?" I asked.

"Yes, I am," she replied, with a smile. "How about you?"

"Me too. I try to give myself a good day, every day," I said, smiling back.

Joanie's expression changed. She looked at me quite seriously. "You're lucky honey. All my life I didn't know it was my job to make myself happy, not until now.

I thought it was my job to take care of everyone else; make *them* happy. And you know what? It never worked." She gave herself a good belly chuckle, shrugged her shoulders, and said, "I wish I'd known sooner. I would have had a better life. Not that it was bad; it wasn't. I just would have been happier, I think. I would have had more joy and fun, been more relaxed."

Joanie's right. To know that you're responsible for all the happiness you'll ever have is the secret to a satisfying life. The sooner you understand that, the better.

I asked Joanie why she didn't do more to make herself happy.

Her response: "I didn't know I could. I didn't know I had the right to put my own happiness and myself first in my life. I was busy with all of my roles and responsibilities. I was a mother, wife, daughter, teacher, choir member, community member, friend – you name it. I was always busy serving others, making sure they had what they needed and were happy."

Again, she laughed her belly laugh, resigned to what she had created. "There was no room left for me and what I really wanted." She closed her eyes and put her head against the back of the chair.

"No room left for me…" A life of doing for others, but with no room left for Self. What caused Joanie to turn away from her Self? What led her to give her energy and life force to everyone but herself?

When Average No Longer Fits

Just as we buy into LIES about who we are as individuals, we also accept many of the customs we witness among members of our cultural groups. *Taught and bought*, we manifest LIES common to cultural groups with whom we identify. In these groups, we find people with whom we share a common history and worldview. While we're not all alike, there are important commonalties.

Then, for a brief moment, we glimpse the possibility that this way of thinking and being – our way – no longer suits us. Such a moment is another *Pivot Point*, a time to turn and move in a different direction. So it was for Sam, my father.

Sam drank heavily and chain-smoked from the time he was a teenager. According to him, "Everyone around me was doing it, so I did it too. I didn't know any better. Years later, I realized I had ruined my life and health. Then, I decided to make a change."

At forty-seven years old, like a suit he had outgrown, the norms he knew no longer worked for him. He decided to shift the way he lived. Others in his group remained enmeshed in unhealthy habits, but Sam searched for a way out. With determination, he released himself from damaging and detrimental habits. For Sam, average no longer fit. "The decision to change, and meaning it, was the hardest part," he said. That's the first big hurdle for most: deciding and meaning it.

Not Belonging

When you decide to leave the space – the mental and emotional space – you once occupied, you'll have to deal with the feeling of not belonging where there was once a perfect fit. Matt said, "Once I became serious about advancing my career, I didn't feel right in certain situations. I even had to find a new lunch group. I felt different about everything and had to make a new place for myself. The old one just didn't work anymore."

How do you quell the fear-based question, "Who am I if I'm not who I used to be?" Lawrence faced this challenge. "I didn't know what to do after my wife died. I didn't fit anywhere or with anyone. Our friends were couples and I'm not a couple...not any longer. Who am I? I don't know. What am I to do? I'm not sure."

Uncertainty and the unfamiliar cause us to live in ambiguity – in the not knowing. Eventually the ground settles and once again, you have a more fixed sense of "this is where I am." Allow the change process to unfold. Give yourself time and space to let change move at the pace it needs and you need. *The Border Patrol* will use your fear of ambiguity to call you back to the "safety" of the old place. Don't be fooled. There's no security in being less than you are. There's no safety in being in a place where you don't belong – a place that robs you of vitality and purpose.

Recognize the ways the call comes from within to follow the high road to your original destiny. For example, if you look at your life and think any of the following, the high road is calling your name:

- "I [insert the particular action], but I don't like it anymore."
- "I don't feel good about myself when I [insert the particular behavior]."
- "I can't explain it, but I want to [insert the particular behavior *change*]."

Change is calling your name – change for good.

Journal Your Truth

How much attention do you pay to what others think and say?

In what way do you allow public opinion to curtail your freedom?

What stories have you made up about them — what they're thinking and saying — that influence your choices?

Do you labor under the same LIES as Joanie?

Which "important roles" take precedence over attention to your Self?

If you were freed from these "roles" what would you do for your Self?

Where in your life are you held hostage by a damaging and detrimental Self-concept?

Where in your life have you compromised who you are and what you stand for in order to fit into a group — family, friends, colleagues, cultural group?

What has it cost you?

Chapter Eleven

The Quest

❦

What's in Your Way?

What's in the way of changing for good and accessing to your true nature? LIES dull the connection to your calling and make you afraid of the truth of who you are. You fear losing what you've worked hard for. You fear being challenged about your beliefs and choices.

You don't begin life alienated from your Spirit and Purpose, and it doesn't always end that way, but the intervening years can be a challenge. That is the time when you have to wake up to the *LIES That Limit* you and confront the controlling, sabotaging power of *The Border Patrol*. Identify the LIES in your life, and ultimately learn how to let them go, setting your Self free.

She Did and You Can Too

Like Melanie in St. Thomas, you can choose in favor of your heart's desire, even in the face of naysayers. Melanie had her detractors and you'll have yours. Her parents didn't want her wasting the investment of a college education or getting behind schedule in building her career. Family and friends didn't want her moving so far away from home. All of that matters, in a way. It's all an expression of their love for her. And it's also a story of their fears about undesired consequences and unknown outcomes.

Wisely, Melanie listened to her Self – to her inner voice, her Spirit. She's happy with her decision and the life she's created. That's what makes life meaningful – listening to the guidance you receive from Spirit and following the Purpose and plan within you.

Listen to your inner voice as it says, "Yes. *This* is right for me, now. *This* is what I want." These are the moments when intuition discerns and communicates what the heart desires, and action planning backed by courage and determination will help make it happen, even in the face of strong opposition from others.

Who Do They Love?

The trouble with LIES is not only do they limit access to the truth of who you are, they also distort perceptions about what you have a right to. What was once a whole person feels reduced to something smaller, less significant, and fragmented. Those who taught you the Labels, Illusions, Excuses, and Stories view you as perfectly normal now that you believe. You, like them, are reduced to average size, living under the control of a power other than your own truth.

Raised right and carefully taught, you now know the way to think and behave – the right customs and traditions to follow – the right mask to wear. Now, you share a belief system that encourages you to avoid a deep connection with your inner Self. It causes you to question the validity of your desires and deny your right to full power and authority over your life. In return for a false sense of safety and belonging, you give up independent thought and action. You determine to blend in and not stand out for fear that *they* will cut down the tall poppy. You can't, you won't risk losing their love and approval.

But who do they love? Of whom do they approve? Certainly, not *you*. *You* are not there, not any longer. *You* disappeared when you unwittingly traded away your authenticity.

I feel loved when I am real with others. Then, if they choose to love and accept me, it's the real me they're embracing. When you own your experience and respectfully say what you think, how you feel, and what's important to you, you validate and value your Self. You're not being political, polite, or poisonous. You're just being honest with your Self about yourself. Does this sound selfish? Do you worry about offending others? Offense is possible, especially if you're speaking LIES.

LIES stimulate and perpetuate blame, shame, guilt, fear, and anger – all negative emotions and attitudes bound together to create distance between you and your real Self and between you and others. It's almost guaranteed that you'll offend and be seen as selfish if you mistake speaking your truth for spewing negativity. Truth is a clarifier and peacemaker. It bears the banner of integrity.

When you speak truth, allowing others to know the real you, you say how you feel without blaming anyone or anything. For example, if you're angry, you could say, "Right now, I'm reacting with anger. I want to work through my angry feelings before we talk. Now is not a good time for me to discuss this with you." Or you could say, "Given what happened, I feel embarrassed and ashamed." The point is you're speaking honestly, demonstrating respect for yourself and others.

LIES would have you hold others responsible for your feelings: "they" made you mad; "they" hurt your feelings; "they" disrespected you. LIES disempower and discourage accountability.

To be honest and nontoxic, you have to do important work, the end-goal of which is to take full responsibility for what you think, how you feel, and how you react to every situation in your life. The process is straightforward. The challenge comes in disentangling your thoughts, feelings, and reactions from the emotional roots of your automatic reflex response. It's not automatic; you don't have to respond the way you do, though you may feel you have no choice. Fact is you can make a conscious choice if you slow down and attend to your inner process. This process will lead to effective self-management. Doing so requires *conscious commitment* and vigilance.

Here's how to change your reaction and speak your truth in a situation where you think you might offend. First, consciously commit to not act on your first reaction the moment something occurs. Your new responsibility is to take time to *intentionally reflect* on what has happened. Notice the thoughts that come to mind and the feelings that follow. Become familiar with the sequence *ACTIONS – THOUGHTS – FEELINGS – REACTIONS*, if you want to share the real you, without blame, shame, intended offense, or injury to others. Slow down enough to see each part of your internal, lightening quick, process in detail.

Make a *conscious choice and commitment* to communicate your truth with integrity and respect for yourself and others. While it's a challenge to move from your habituated pattern of reflex response to the new way, it is possible. You can do it, if you choose to. If you take that step, you and everyone around you will have greater awareness of your authentic Self, not just your familiar, practiced mask.

So, maybe the question is not, "Who do *they* love," but rather, "Who do *you* love?" Think about it. You project out onto others and ask the world to give you what you really want for yourself.

When *you* love you, you relate to yourself with compassion. You'll relate without the fear of losing another's love or approval. You'll courageously share your authentic Self. You are your gift to you and to them. When it comes to genuine relationship, genuine interaction, and genuine communication, make your Self your first focus, the object of your attention, compassion, and commitment.

When I suffer — feel lonely, overwhelmed, unloved, overworked, undervalued, exhausted, not understood and appreciated — I have disconnected from the power of my truth. I've stopped being real, transparent with my Self. No wonder I don't feel loved if the real me is not there to be loved. Without my honest presence I'm unavailable for love. At my command, an imposter sits in my place. To feel and be loved, I have to expose the real me. First, I have to be sincere and honest with my Self, so that I have access to the real me. Then, I make a *conscious choice* to let my Spirit be seen and loved — by me and everyone else.

Your core must be seen and loved by others if you are to be and feel known, understood, and appreciated. In order to feel authentic and be in harmony with your truth, you must live true to your Purpose. Become your own lover. Give yourself the love and honor you deserve. When you live in alignment with your Spirit and Purpose, you give your Self the love and honor you long for. Then the love and appreciation you receive from others will be received and experienced as credible. You will be filled from the inside out. Perhaps for the first time in your life, you will be "it" — the earthly embodiment and manifestation of love. That's the grand mission you're called to, Spirit of Purpose.

Underneath the Quilting Rack

When I was in my mid-thirties, my father told me "From the time you were a small child, you used to say, 'I'm going to make the world a better place.'"

That idea just seemed to be in me, naturally. It's not something anyone taught me. Whenever I think about making the world a better place, I feel excited. It's as if a spark goes off in me, igniting flames. I feel a surge of power and passionate energy in my gut — a knowing.

Today, I still believe I'm here to contribute positively to the world, to make it a better place. First and foremost, that process begins with how I think about and treat myself, by virtue of how I live and interact with others and the world around me.

Deeply understanding my Self and comprehending the uniqueness of others is my passion. As a child, I sat and listened to adults talk. I enjoyed connecting with them and discerning what they were feeling. I loved hearing what they had to say and understanding the world from their perspective. Lost in my communion with them, I would be called back to the moment by Mom or Granny. One or the other would tell me to, "Go outside and play. Stop looking in grown people's mouths." A little embarrassed at being caught and called out, I would go out to find my brother or play alone.

Today, listening and seeing people for who they really are — seeing their Spirit and Purpose — is one of my core competencies. Able to perceive and understand deeply, I grasp the spoken message and sense in the silences the emotional roots of the speaker's message. I hear what is said and what's left unsaid. This ability is strongly connected to my Purpose.

To know another deeply — at their core — is to love them. This is also required if you are to love your Self. Listening helps me take in others — see and accept them for who they are and what they're expressing and experiencing. No matter the story they share or the image they project, I see their greatness, their Spirit and Purpose — the gifts they were born to bring to the world. While their ego may distort, even obstruct, their knowledge of themselves, I take pleasure in seeing and connecting with their core, their beauty as Spirit. It's rewarding to affirm whatever aspects of their passion and Purpose I glimpse.

Granny, her sister Mary, her sisters-in-law Ossie, Elise, and Marion were quilters. In the fall, after all the crops were in, they would gather at one or the other's house, each bringing a dish of something to share, and spend the day quilting. There, in conversation, they made themselves vulnerable, patched up one another's wounds, and stitched together bonds of sisterhood that endured until they died. I was privileged to sit underneath the quilting rack, quietly out of sight, forgotten by the women as they talked and stitched; turning mere rags into beautiful works of art and comforting warmth for the people they loved.

Sitting in stillness and silence, on the cool unfinished wood floor, I listened to them talk about their problems, pray for each other and each other's children, laugh together, and admire each other's creative talents as mothers, quilters, and cooks. Many of the lessons learned, while literally sitting at their feet, are with me today. One such life lesson was about the necessity and power of unconditional love and upholding the Purpose and potential of those they loved.

Whether their pain was precipitated by infidelity, the anguish of a child "turned bad," betrayal in a friendship, or wondering when the Lord would deliver them or those for whom they prayed, they always loved – no matter what.

They loved and supported each other. They forgave the unforgivable. One might say to the other, "You can be sure, in his heart he didn't know what he was doing. If he did, he wouldn't have done that." Another might add, "You can't blame a person for what they do when they ain't clothed in their right-mind."

I took in their words. While I didn't expressly understand the terms they used, I captured and integrated into my being the energy and intention locked in their sentences, and the way they chuckled and laughed, breathed or sighed, even moaned and cried, as they spoke.

These wonderful women looked beyond the prideful posturing and destructive tendencies of the people around them. They looked to and did all they could to call forth the core – the constructive and loving nature of those around them. They did their best to nurture the spiritual nature and ignite the flame that burned – dimly or brightly – inside the hearts of their loved ones.

From Mom, Granny, and those great women, I learned that love is the only truth that can safely guide your life; forgiveness is a necessary component of love; and when a person behaves badly, see their behavior as a mistake. Understand he or she is not "clothed in their right-mind." Look beyond the present action and consider what shaped the person. What *Pivot Points* led to the poor choice? Then, encourage change.

Much later I learned that these lessons were spiritual principles; principles those women used to steer their lives away from LIES – Labels, Illusions, Excuses, and Stories – and limitations on their capacity to love and nurture. These same concepts are at the core of my life today – all learned while sitting underneath the quilting rack, eavesdropping on Granny and her "girls."

Listening compassionately, in stillness and silence, continues to be one of my greatest passions. It enables me to fulfill my purpose – to help myself and others peel away the mask and uncover the truth of who we really are – the truth of our loving, authentic core essence.

The Quest

In nearly thirty years of working with talented and successful people, I have found few who feel whole. Most feel something is missing, they are incomplete; there is a hole somewhere in their inner tube.

Fragmented, critical of Self and others, they project a level of confidence they don't feel. Longing for a calmer mind, clarity in decision-making, and a fuller sense of self-satisfaction, they would love to resolve the emotional angst that disturbs their peace. Instead of feeling the hole, they want to be whole.

The fact is, it was trained out of you and me, primarily with the intent of providing loving guidance and protection. Distortions are like that, deceitful at every turn. The good news is you and I can reclaim awareness of our wholeness and perfection, if we commit to the quest.

Journal Your Truth

Who do you believe is your true, authentic Self?

Do you allow others to see and love the real you?

How do you cover over your true Self?

Exercise

Write down five things you love about yourself.

What qualities exist in others that you admire and believe are worth emulating?

What are the top three things you think cause you to feel unloved?

Which of those things are LIES, misconceptions?

Which of those things can you change or stop holding on to?

What can you do to motivate yourself to really commit to making changes, letting go of the LIES that limit you?

Chapter Twelve

LIES Detector Tools

☯

The Right Tools

Unlike most trips where you carry baggage, this trip — your journey to greater self-awareness, a deeper connection with your Spirit, and a growing willingness to manifest your purpose — is one where you shed baggage. Its purpose is the release of all that holds you back, weighs you down, suppresses your Spirit, oppresses your purpose, and limits your freedom to be you. Ideally, the tools you carry won't be cumbersome or complicated. They need to be simple, functional, and effective — easily accessible.

When you journey into the land guarded by *The Border Patrol,* you need a good map and the right tools — the right mindset and self-management techniques — to confront it, sweet talk it, charm it, ignore it, and get beyond its perimeter. When you make the decision to free yourself from the grips your mental manager and guardian of the LIES — the one who restricts your ability to know who you really are and do what you were born to do — your primary job will be self-management, being aware of and in charge of your thoughts, feelings, actions, and reactions.

Accountability becomes your watchword, your mantra, one of your key goals. Detecting and dismantling the LIES in your life will result in a greater sense of personal freedom and accountability for making your life exactly as you want it to be. You'll feel and be empowered to accurately analyze situations and your response. You'll have the clarity and presence of mind to make better decisions and own the consequences of your choices and actions. With accountability comes greater personal power. Who can argue with that result?

One set of tools you can utilize to enhance your level of self-awareness is a process I call *intentional reflection* and *conscious choice.*

It will help you gain the clarity and strength to keep moving forward toward a real relationship with your core essence and reason for being. The pairing and consistent utilization of these two techniques results in *transformational change*.

Intentional Reflection and Conscious Choice

Uncovering the LIES in your life takes you on an inward journey. A willingness to look inward and engage in *intentional reflection* will position you to make mindful, *conscious choices*. The combination – *intentional reflection and conscious choice* – will lead to outcomes more aligned with your deepest desires.

When you employ *intentional reflection*, you will: be thoughtful and purposeful about what you do and how you do it; understand the reasons behind the choices you make; notice the gap between what you desire and what actually happens; examine the impact of your actions; and make adjustments so your life gets better and better.

All too often our behavior is defined by reflex reactions to people and situations. *Intentional reflection* enables us to make *conscious choices*, making it possible to move beyond the parameters set by our social programming – the mind-training that occurs within cultural clans, families, and the broader society.

What's involved in the process of *intentional reflection and conscious choice?* There are five *Pivot Points* to consider and apply that will help you move more masterfully in the direction of your desires. They will help you pivot in a positive direction. As you open your heart and mind, these five *Pivot Points* involved in *intentional reflection* and *conscious choice* can lead to *transformational change* – a remarkable shift in your way of seeing and being.

1. *Look within and analyze the situation you've decided to change.*
    Consider your contribution to the current condition of the situation. Become familiar with the places in your mind where you are split, in discord. Your mind may say one thing and your emotions another.

2. *Reflect on the content of your mind <u>and</u> emotions.*

   Notice what you're thinking, how you're feeling and what you're saying to yourself and others. Look, sense, and listen for the LIES — the Labels, Illusions, Excuses, and Stories — that are playing out in your thoughts, feelings, conversations, and ultimately, your actions. The resulting circumstances of your life give good hints about the content and conflict of your mind and emotions.

3. *Make conscious choices.*

   Understand your full range of options. Look for ways to expand the spectrum of possibilities. When you get your thoughts and feelings — your energy and attitude — in sync with your goal and intentions, solutions and opportunities will show up. That's the way the universe works.

4. *Test the sincerity and credibility of your commitment.*

   Are you fully committed to the choice you've made? Or, does the goal just sound like a good idea, or seem like something you *should* do? Is there alignment between your stated goal or intention and your real thoughts, feelings, and beliefs? Do all levels of your conversations — the ones you think <u>and</u> the ones you articulate — match your goal and the actions you're considering? If so, you're congruent and harmonious; your energy and intentions, your head and heart are operating on the same plane. Congruent thoughts and feelings are a necessary component of commitment.

5. *Hold yourself accountable for achieving your goal.*

   When you feel yourself working counter to your intention — take full responsibility for getting back on track. Blame no one, not even yourself. There is no need to be self-critical or feel sorry for yourself. If you have a day of failure or forgetting, frustration or fatigue, simply start over. If your commitment is authentic, you'll find new and creative ways to be faithful to your Self and continue moving toward your goal — toward knowing and living a life that is consistent with the deep urgings of your Spirit.

Look and Listen for LIES

If you haven't yet begun to question the falsehoods in your life, begin now. Clear up the misconceptions that have been controlling you. Once you arrive at this life-changing decision and commit to unmasking the delusions you count as fact, you'll be released and truth will be revealed.

Begin looking and listening for assumptions. Catch yourself as you use common phrases and clichés; things you have often said, spoken as absolute truth. Ask yourself: *"Is this truth — true always, without exception — or am I repeating without thought what I've heard and said thousands of times?"*

Bigger LIES, *Grand Design LIES*, and insidious assumptions will become apparent. You'll hear a statement and questions will occur to you:

- *"This sounds true. But, is it truth?"*
- *"Do you really mean, <u>always</u>? Are there no exceptions?"*
- *"'They' won't let you? Who are 'they'? What have you tried?"*

Challenge your assumptions with, "Wait a minute. Does it *have* to be this way?"

Learning to Recognize LIES – The Ordinary Is Extraordinary

LIES live in day-to-day ordinary moments. But, their impact can be extraordinary. They don't appear at certain times. They don't have special and unique hiding places. They don't come out only on holidays or special occasions. Labels, Illusions, Excuses, and Stories are just a part of most conversations we have and interactions we share with others.

It's extraordinary to realize something that has no basis in fact serves as the basis for judgments and decision-making. LIES wield such power in ordinary and extraordinary relationships, situations, and places.

We easily see the negative effect of Labels, Illusions, Excuses, and Stories in others' lives and situations in which we're not directly involved. It's more challenging to see their presence and power over our own lives; but we must if we are to overcome the spell they cast.

Since LIES are taught and reinforced through everyday exchanges, that's the place to look when you're ready to identify them. Constantly, your life gives you feedback about the *LIES That Limit* you. Whenever you feel you're working against yourself, nothing is going right, or you're uneasy about what's happening, LIES may be at work. Look a little more deeply and you're likely to find mind-training at work – thoughts and ideas used by *The Border Patrol* to keep you confined to your comfort zone and away from the joy and satisfaction of being true to your Spirit.

Many people think they must go through complex shenanigans and wail and gnash their teeth to discover what's wrong with them; what's wrong with their life. I say, just look within. Look at the stuff of your everyday life. There lays the answer. Devon's story makes the point.

Actively job-hunting for more than three years, Devon has a great resume, a 30-second branding speech, and networked constantly. He seemed to do all the right things, so he was mystified that he had not found suitable work. As we talked, he simultaneously expressed frustration about his situation and appreciation for freedom from what he called the "9 to 5 corporate grind." He wanted no part of that life again.

Devon's first task was to be honest with himself. Through a series of conversations, he acknowledged the previously unacknowledged. Truth was, he said, "I want to do something I love, something more meaningful than simply working for the money." Good! When truth is spoken, it breaks the grip of LIES and doors open.

Working on his own behalf, Devon created an inventory of his experiences, including professional and volunteer activities. From that, he developed a comprehensive list of his accomplishments, skills, and abilities. Then he gave thought to what he loved doing, what he felt passionate about and would do joyfully even if he received no pay. The answer: he loved working with children. He was a Sunday school teacher and, even as a child, he played teacher. This acknowledgement released him to openly pursue his passion.

Within weeks, Devon landed his first job in the teaching profession as a long-term substitute. Over time, he received the required certifications and became a full-time teacher, and later, a guidance counselor. He helped youngsters shape their careers, encouraging them to go for what they loved. He was an authentic witness for the value of finding what you love and making that your life's work.

LIES originate and are reinforced daily through conversations; observation of others; reading newspapers, magazines, blogs, and books; or watching movies and television. As readily as the truth is accepted, so are beliefs and traditions that sound true and simply are not. Each of us plays a critical part in accepting and perpetuating the false ideas and illusions that rob us of the freedom to have the life that is rightfully ours.

You might say, "Come on Teressa. How on earth would I choose to perpetuate something that takes away my joy?" The direct answer is: You do it whenever you buy in to LIES, and continuously validate the limiting assumption while ignoring data to the contrary. Furthermore, you expend energy silencing and dismissing inner wisdom that tells you, "This isn't the truth. Wait. Think again. Something here is not right." No matter what the distortion, you play an active part in its existence.

One such example that affected my life for a long time was an idea I heard over and over again. It's probably one you've heard too. It's the myth of meritocracy. Trusting the advice to work hard, keep my head down and my nose clean, I believed if I did so, I would get my due. That was an illusion, a partial truth – a common cultural story about how to get ahead. That's not exactly the way it works for people who achieve big goals and create a path to their passion.

Merit matters in that it makes you credible and demonstrates your expertise – your technical ability to do what's expected. But, for many people whose efforts warrant recognition, promotion, or elevation, it doesn't happen.

Experience has shown me that the truth is more akin to the virtue of working hard and doing the right thing is the baseline; it's your foundation, and nothing more than that. What the well-meaning, "work hard and keep your nose clean" advice doesn't point out is that focusing on merit alone blinds you to the full range of what is needed to get ahead in a world that is more subjective and relational than most would care to admit.

This teaching left me ignorant of the value and power of having a clear vision and talking about it. I needed to have high expectations and share bold dreams, aggressively network with people who can and will help me advance my agenda by opening doors, and take necessary risks.

I've met countless people who, like me, bought in to LIES such as this one. LIES are like brainwashing. They interfere with our ability to see how things really work. We just believe the story we were told, time and again. The message becomes a trusted a guide we live by, despite the fact it doesn't result in the outcome we want.

Once you've done the work to connect with your Spirit and the Purpose you were born to fulfill, asking for what you want will become easier. You'll have a legitimate reason for asking. In fact, your higher Self will guide your requests. Such requests are not selfish or self-serving. They tend to serve a positive purpose and benefit more than the person making the request. Your higher Self helps you connect with your higher Purpose. Your higher Purpose serves you and does no harm to anyone else.

From this perspective, asking is backed by a sense of mission, not entitlement and ego-fulfillment. To be clear, this does not mean you don't have to be strategic and thoughtful about who you ask and what you ask for. You do. And, if you practice *intentional reflection* and *conscious choice*, the right request and the optimal approach will be made clear. You'll receive some level of clear guidance or inspiration that lets you know, "Do or say this. Do or say it this way." With selfish self-interest aside, you can ask with a sense of deserving because what you want serves a higher good. That means it's good for you and it benefits others.

Study Your Stories

LIES are reflected in the stories you hear, tell, and read. And, here's the kicker: You *choose* to ignore or discount information contrary to the LIES. You accept data that perpetuates the misguided thinking that limits your options and potential.

Study the stories you choose to tell and retell to uncover the LIES that you allow to limit your life. Are they positive, affirming stories or negative and diminishing? In your stories, are you the heroine or the victim? Telling them, how do you feel — fearful and nervous or strengthened and courageous? Do you tell tales about your vision for the life you want to live, or about the unsatisfying life you're living and why you long to leave it behind?

A colleague told me, "At the end of the day, my husband's stories are about the things he did well. He's the hero, the smart one. My stories relay the way I fell short of my expectations, what I did wrong and who annoyed me. Is he boasting or am I depressed and defeated?" Which of them is living LIES?

If both are sincere in what they say, perhaps the person who is free of negative Labels, Illusions, Excuses, and Stories is the one who feels most positive, clear minded, uplifted, and centered. Complaining can help you feel unburdened, but it won't lift your spirits, allowing you to soar.

Imagine what might happen, how you might feel, if you let go of the negative stories and assumptions you've allowed to erode your self-confidence and positive outlook. Begin challenging the thoughts you think and the words you speak. The next time you have a recurring thought or make a statement you've made a thousand times before, stop and ask yourself: "Is this what I was taught to believe and accept, or is this truth?"

The impact of LIES is often so subtle you may think, "What's the big deal? I don't have these issues."

Well, that's precisely what makes LIES so treacherous — you don't believe they affect *you*. You don't realize they're hiding out, operating beneath your conscious awareness, influencing your thoughts and choices, manifesting in your behavior. So, how do you know when LIES are at work in your belief system?

One clue about the influence of LIES in your life is to look at your pattern of choices and consequences. Wherever you find less than satisfactory results you're probably face-to-face with some version of a Label, Illusion, Excuse, or Story.

The tricky thing about LIES is they are true *sometimes*, but we treat them as if they are absolute truth. There is a difference between LIES and truth.

The Difference Between LIES and Truth

The difference between LIES and the truth is simple: *truth is always true*. Labels, Illusions, Excuses, and Stories are true sometimes, and sometimes not. In my view, if there is an exception, you don't have a rule. It's not a universal, immutable fact. It's just a culturally accepted notion.

Bigger than the limits of popular opinion, scientific knowledge, cultural tradition, or the understanding of religious leaders, real truth is amazing, often unfathomable, unchanging reality. Truth applies to everyone equally, all the time. For example, the law of gravity has no favorites. It treats everyone under the same conditions, the same way. The laws of abundance don't discriminate. The laws of quantum physics and energy are unchanging. As science advances we may understand the laws differently, but the laws themselves – whether known to us or yet to be discovered – never change. That's what I call truth.

The existence of Spirit is truth. It's a fact that never changes, no matter what you or I believe. You can choose not to believe in Spirit, or to believe whole-heartedly. It doesn't matter. The fact of its existence remains. You are Spirit. Your spiritual energy has taken up residence in a physical body for a time, for a reason. When that time is over, and your purpose fulfilled, the energy that animated your body leaves the physical, material vessel behind. Disrobed, your Spirit moves back into a state of pure being, pure energy.

I've come to believe that very little of what we call truth is actually true. Much of it is just the action of probability and belief. If a thing happens to enough people, we call it fact. If it happens to a lot of people, the probability of its reoccurrence increases as more and more people begin to believe it. Belief activates it, making it seem more real than it is. It's not an undeniable, nonnegotiable fact. Accurately viewed, it's a widely held belief.

You and I would be freer if only we would release ourselves from the stranglehold of the myths, dysfunctional traditions, and false beliefs we allow to define our thoughts, moods, decisions, and actions. If you were without thoughts that impede your progress, slow your evolution, and block access to the fulfillment of healthy desire, you would be more in alignment with your unique Spirit of Purpose. The joy of doing what you love and fulfilling your calling would be your daily experience. Much of the longing, frustration, and grasping for what turns out to be nothing would cease. Claiming and creating a better, more satisfying way of living, you would have a renewed sense of peace.

When you reach for inner wisdom, the answers you've long searched for are made plain. Uncover your answers – the ones that are right specifically for you – and you will develop the courage to do the very thing you are here to learn and contribute.

Here is a **Four-Step Test for Truth**. I use it and recommend it to clients. It's helpful when you want to discern truth from falsehood. As you face a situation and need to respond, ask yourself: Is what I'm about to say or do...

1. *Based on fear or any other negative emotion? If so, your response is not aligned with truth. It's based on LIES and limits.*

2. *Going to disrespect or diminish me, or others involved? If so, it is a distortion based on LIES and limits.*

3. *Creating or sustaining unnecessary limitations for me or others? If so, it is a LIES-based myth.*

4. *Inhibiting healthy Self-expression – mine or others? If so, it is a false idea based on LIES and designed to limit.*

Dreams Can Be Teachers

The importance of dreams as teachers has been known and respected for ages, particularly by many religious and spiritual traditions, as well as psychologists, psychiatrists, visionaries, and mystics. For our purposes of self-discovery and self-empowerment, I'll show you how to make great use of them.

Dreams are magical windows into multiple dimensions of the mind and heart. I pay close attention to mine and encourage you to do the same with yours. Dreams are teachers. Rising up to consciousness from the subconscious mind, they can help you see what's *really* troubling you; how you're actually feeling; what you're refusing to face or own; and what you're longing for. Dreams can provide insight into your past and present, or a glimpse into a potential future. Rich in imagery and feeling, dreams hold valuable information.

If you'd like to learn more about dream interpretation, buy a few books and read the perspective of different authors. Try out the suggested approaches to determine which system feels most right and useful. Or, take a dream interpretation workshop. Many current authors offer in-person learning opportunities. Having taken dream interpretation workshops, I know they can be educational and fun.

As I mentioned in Chapter One, I am not an authority in dream interpretation for anyone but myself. Using Percept Language, the technique I described in that chapter, my dreams prove to be a rich source of information, particularly information I haven't yet allowed into my conscious awareness. Dreams help me tap into my unconscious – a gold mine of treasure about the parts of me I know well, and those parts that live in the secret recesses of my mind.

To recap, Percept encourages you to see and describe all parts of your dream, animate and inanimate, as parts of you, owning the idea that each character or element exists in you. The technique can be incredibly illuminating when applied to dreams or any situation. Percept helps me own the meaning I give to everything I experience, acknowledging that the real action and reaction is in me – in my head and heart, not out there in the world.

When I think in Percept terms, I am the doer and creator of my life experience, moment to moment, based on how I perceive and think about the world around and within me. This way, I become keenly aware that *reality* is in me.

For my purposes here, I've simplified the method I learned from the Weirs and Alexandra Merrill. The basic approach I take to applying Percept to my dreams, and frankly to situations in my daily life, includes the following:

- I add the statement, "part of me," after I name any character or significant object in my dream – every noun and pronoun. If we go back to my dream about India, described in Chapter One, I can talk about the five-year-old part of me; the travel companion part of me; the older, wise woman part of me; *The Border Patrol* part of me; the free part of me; etc.

- At times, I use the statement, "in me" instead of using the words, "part of me." In either case, the language helps me see each of these characters or objects as parts of me. In doing so I can explore the images, ideas, and feelings I have about these aspects in me. I can see how these parts, known or unknown, are in me. Substituting "in me" for "parts of me," using the above examples, I would examine the five-year-old in me; the travel companion in me; the older, wise woman in me; etc.

- Though not described in Chapter One, but consistent with the application of Percept, another important step I took with the dream involved using language in a way that made me the central actor and perceiver of everything. For example, in regular speech, I might say, "It was so scary to face *The Border Patrol*." When using Percept, "it" or "this" or "that" is changed to "I" or "me," and the active form of all verbs is used. The intent is to enable you to see yourself as the doer of all you experience. Instead of saying, "It was frightening to face to *The Border Patrol*," I say, "I frighten me with *The Border Patrol* in me." Or, "I frighten me with *The Border Patrol* part of me."

Do you get the impact of Percept Language? I find it powerful and eye-opening. Oops. Let me Percept this part of me. "I am the power in me." Or, "I am the powerful, eye-opening part of me."

By the way, if you're feeling a little confused or overwhelmed right now, don't believe those LIES. You can get this. Play with Percept Language and see what this technique enables you to reveal to yourself about the many known and unknown parts of you. Using dreams and Percept, you may discover aspects of yourself that have been holding up your progress for years. More aware of your internal saboteurs and *Border Patrol*, you'll have a clearer perception about new ways to have power over your experience.

Become a Keen Self-Observer

Keen self-observation is a critical self-awareness skill. We're accustomed to noticing others, often in detail. We watch what they do and try to figure them out. Are they sincere and trustworthy? Do they seem committed to the idea they're putting forth? We guess about their degree of self-confidence based on what we observe when interacting with them. We try to get inside of their minds to see their thoughts, anticipate their next move, or make an educated guess about their needs and wants. We like to think we know what makes them tick.

You're probably a keen observer of others. It's an important skill to have, if you want to be effective. Keen observation of others enables you to have empathy; you understand their competencies and challenges. It supports strategic thinking and effective decision-making. It's a tool that helps you communicate influentially and successfully. When you know your audience, you're able to tailor your message so it reaches them and respects their needs and agenda.

Most people, put more attention on noticing what others are doing than they put on themselves. We learn to do so early in life as we try to survive. We learn to watch *them* to determine how we want to respond to get what we want.

Carefully observe any child and you'll see this dynamic play out. The child knows how and when to ask a parent or caregiver for what they want. They know how to choose the time, place, and tone to maximize their chances of a "Yes." The child in each of us is still alive and has a depth of expertise as an observer of others.

So, here's the question: Are you a keen observer of yourself? Do you notice your details? Do watch yourself in action? Do you put energy into discerning what makes you tick? Maybe. Maybe not.

Keen self-observation is essential when you decide to free your Self from the LIES in your life. You'll have to look and listen carefully or you'll miss the subtle ways LIES show up and limit you. This message about the value of self-observation came home for me clearly one day as I exercised.

I was subtly aware of the power of keen self-observation, but that day what had been subtle became significant.

I exercise because of how I feel when it's over. I feel great! But I can slack off gearing up to begin, and then following through with the level of perfection that would serve me best.

Executing any routine, whether it's a front kick, an overhead pull-down, bicep curls, or a plank, I can fool myself, happily. I'll do the movement, minus excellent form and execution. I just want to get it over with, that's where my energy is focused.

While I'm in the activity, I'm not really committed to being conscious and doing it correctly. Yet I miss receiving maximal benefit from my effort when I don't perform the movement in the way it was intended. Cheating my way through the process, I cheat myself out of the real results I want.

The same is true of every action you take in life. If you succumb to the illusion of doing it right, you deny yourself the full effect you could enjoy.

Working out with Monica, my trainer, I feel better about my workout and achieve better results. She calls my attention to my posture and positioning. With her powers of keen observation, I don't get away with using improper form or restricting my range of motion to something suboptimal. She helps me make micro-adjustments that make a big difference. With Monica, LIES cannot live.

This book can help you make the micro-movements, small adjustments in your mindset and belief system that will make a difference. Don't allow shoddy work to rob you of your right to be exactly as you want. Put committed effort into whatever you want to experience. Get your energy and intentions, your feelings and actions, aligned. Don't kid yourself, pretending you've done so when you haven't. Work with and for your heart's desires.

Become a keen observer of yourself. Notice what you do and how you do it. Be aware of the energy – mental, emotional, and physical – you put into any activity or plan. Check your form and execution. Are you really committed or are you faking it, trying to look and sound like you're doing the right thing when really you're just making a cursory attempt.

I've done this so many times – feigned effort and intention. I did so because of the *shoulds* rummaging through my head – pressure from *The Border Patrol*. Seldom did any of these half-hearted undertakings ever result in much good; at least none that endured.

When I've been the object of other people's less-than-authentic efforts, I've never wanted what they were offering. I don't feel good receiving something given with a measure of resentment, or a preference to withhold it.

You're withholding from yourself whenever you say you want something – a relationship, a new position, better health, greater wealth and abundance – and you resent the mental, emotional, or physical effort required to bring it to life. You become your own barrier to success when you carry out an action without employing proper form, execution, and follow-through. If you want results, commit and do it right. Get your energy and intentions to agree and work in concert.

Are you living in alignment with your highest and best intentions, your Spirit of Purpose? Or, are you pretending that compromised effort will lead to the positive end you desire? Compromised effort is not committed energy, and won't create the same result as energetic, committed effort.

Aligning Your Energy and Intentions

Throughout the book, you'll notice I ask you to talk with yourself, delivering a certain message or asking specific questions. It's all for a reason. I want you to purposefully reconnect with your Self – your own internal witness and wisdom. Talking with your Self, your Spirit, is the best way to strengthen the relationship and reset negative *Pivot Points* to ones that enable you to banish LIES and reestablish Spirit as your internal authority.

Besides, self-talk is nothing new. You do it all the time. I'm simply asking you to become aware of the dialogue and apply the constructive focus provided to align your energy and intentions.

Over time, I've learned to align my energy or feelings with my intentions or thoughts. This dynamic duo – *aligned energy (feelings)* and *intentions (thoughts)* — helps me stay centered and accomplish my goals. This is the engine that drives manifestation. The key to making this engine run well: *agreement between your head and heart.*

I didn't always know that, and accordingly, I didn't always do that. If I did, it occurred by happenstance. I was left wondering why it was that I tried and tried to accomplish a goal, without success.

When I learned how to align my head and heart, my thoughts and feelings, success came more easily. And, when I didn't accomplish my aim, I had an easier time diagnosing why that was so. I knew that either I didn't believe in what I was doing or I didn't think it was probable. When my thoughts and feelings weren't supporting the creative process, the expected outcome eluded me. A correction had to be made. I had to adjust either how I felt or what I was thinking. My head and heart had to be in agreement to make it all work. The work of aligning my energy and intentions became fun — when it wasn't frustrating or confusing.

Nowadays, if there is something I want to achieve or experience I can usually make it happen. I set a goal, focus on it, discerning what I think about it and how I feel. I create appropriate actions to accomplish it and keep my eyes open for synchronistic events. Nine times out of ten, I get the result I want. If not completely, I end up with most of what I want — at least enough to feel good about my efforts and the results they yielded. Since life is a process of evolution, I move from one goal to the next, working on my long and unending list of ideas and possibilities, options and opportunities.

With that said, I must confess, I still have places in my life where I don't feel powerful or use my full potential. In certain situations, about certain things, or in some relationships, I bump up against a boundary that challenges me. The line, that invisible but palpable border, is in my mind. I know that. It exists for things that are important and those that are inconsequential.

For example, I may want to make a change in where or how I live; network with a new group of people I perceive as high powered and accomplished; ask for a raise or seek out new responsibilities; find ways to improve a relationship by confronting what is not working; step up to a new level of responsibility in my career; write a book or pursue some other goal

I've fantasized about. But, anticipating the change and the consequences involved – the intended and unintended consequences, the imagined and the real – I do nothing. While not where I want to be, I stay in my lane. I choose to limit myself and I constrain my freedom. I don't think about it exactly that way, but that is what I've done. Unconsciously, I've chosen a path that ensures I will not experience what I desire.

Of course I'll convince myself that I've made that decision in reaction to some threatening or practical reality related to the situation. Things like, "The timing is not right. I'll get to it later. I don't know how to go about it," and on and on my excuses go. But, the truth is the boundaries and constraints I believe I'm up against are in my mind; made up and exaggerated by me. I haven't yet tested them; I've only imagined what they are and recoiled at the thought.

Aligning your energy and intentions for positive results requires self-inquiry and self-honesty. Come clean with your Self about the degree to which your thoughts about the matter at hand are in sync with your feelings. To capitalize on the power of thoughts and feelings working in harmony, you'll have to notice subtleties concerning the degree to which they are congruent. When you have a match between how you feel and what you think, you have alignment. For example, if you decide to walk ten miles and you have a positive reaction to the idea and you feel positive emotion just thinking of doing it, you've probably achieved alignment.

If you want to change jobs, you can align your energy and intentions by thinking about what you want – the kind of work you want to do; the leadership style you find most inspiring; qualities you value in colleagues; the kind of organizational culture you prefer; the kinds of rewards you appreciate and want. As you consider your list of wants, if you can think *and* feel positive emotion, without the drain of negative self-talk, it's likely you're aligned and well positioned to achieve your goal.

If you notice can'ts, won'ts, or other fear-based thoughts, you're in the midst of a mismatch. If when you think about the idea you feel incompetent, afraid, insecure, angry, helpless, hopeless, or any other self-limiting feeling, you're misaligned. If your thoughts are affirmative and your feelings are working to the contrary, you're not properly positioned.

When that occurs journal your thoughts and feelings. We'll talk more about journaling in the next section. Get your inner dialogue and images out in the open so you can look at them, question your judgments, challenge your conclusions, develop alternative ideas, and move through emotions that block forward momentum. An effective process for uniting your thoughts and feelings is the transformative combination of journaling and the positive self-talk. Self-talk transforms *Tick-Talk, Tick-Talk.* Constructive self-talk works on two dimensions: what you say in your head *and* what you feel in your heart. Agreement between the two — your head and heart — results in aligned energy and intentions.

Journaling

As mentioned above, journaling is a practical technique for processing and working through your thoughts and feelings. There are numerous approaches to journaling. Today, many women *and* men journal regularly. It's a great stress reliever. Getting your inner dialogue down on paper allows you to see what's taking up space in your mind, robbing you of energy, aching your head, creating confusion, churning in your gut.

Journaling can also be a way to express your creativity, generate brilliant ideas, document your goals and dreams, and write about how you imagine feeling as you live your dreams. Talk about stimulating alignment of your energy and intention; this technique does it.

I have clients whose journals are full of beautiful, soulful poems; are simply words and phrases that described their day; are stories; are drawings that capture their mood, ranging from striking artistic renderings to imaginative stick figures — the form matters not. Self-expression is what's key.

Another client has years of journals, volumes; each full of photos and pictures cut from magazines and newspapers. As she is drawn to or inspired by an image, she cuts it and pastes it in her journal. Sometimes she writes a caption under it or a story about what the image means to her — how it relates to her life at the moment. She says, "It's my therapy and relaxation. I've worked out problems and survived relationship crises by pasting pictures on a page. I can look back over a week, a month, or several years and know where I was emotionally and spiritually. The pictures tell the story."

Gratitude journals are also popular these days, and for good reason. They call you to regularly write down what you're grateful for — from the least to the largest. Nothing is off limits. Gratitude journals help you focus on the positive. They provide a physical place to post all that's good in your life, all you're grateful for, including the trials and tribulations that lead you to your growing edge and help you to become more of who you really are.

Your journal is a place where you can empty out, release the restraints, and abandon your baggage and the LIES that live in your head. On paper, LIES can be easier to spot, confront, and change.

People journal in different ways. Some write whatever comes to mind, be it a little or a lot. Others pose a question and write what bubbles up to the surface in response. Still others put the pen against the paper and begin writing, not stopping until they satisfy the goal of a specific number of pages or until a time objective is met. This method suggests you write without stopping, even if you run out of words to write. If that happens, it's suggested you write, "I've run out of things to write." Or, "I can't think of what to write. I wonder what I should write?" Usually, words return and the redundancy ends.

Your approach to journaling is, naturally, something for you to decide. If your current practice works, keep at it. If you'd like to try something new, do it. I've used Julia Cameron's *The Artist's Way* process for a number of years. Her book is a good read and the process is valuable.

Above all, your journal is your private property, never to be shared, unless you choose to do so. Keep it tucked away, out of view, saving prying eyes and curious minds from temptation. Most people say they feel less vulnerable when their private thoughts remain private, unless they make the conscious choice to share them. Be proactive. Create the quality of privacy you need. Then, write away. Bare your soul to your Self. This is territory off limits to *The Border Patrol*. No censoring. Freely express yourself, all parts of you.

Think Inclusively

I've had the pleasure of working with and befriending many great people. Among them is Bill Woodson. One of the things I learned from him is the impact of binary thinking versus inclusive thinking. One is limiting, the other liberating.

The concept is simple: when we think in terms of either/or, we're engaged in binary thinking. We believe I can do this or that. I can have this or that. One choice excludes its opposite.

When we think inclusively, we're able to consider a wider range of possibilities. We see that we can have *both* this *and* that; we can do *both* this *and* that. No option or possibility is automatically excluded because the other exits. Standing together, side-by-side, both contenders for our favor, loyalty and attention can become part of our experience. We may select some of both.

This concept – the value of both/and, inclusive thinking – is very important because most of us trap ourselves with binary, either/or thinking. We limit what we allow ourselves to experience because we think we must choose one thing over another. We limit our knowledge of the wide range of our potential because we think we can do only a narrow range of things; we must live within tight boundaries. *The Border Patrol* reinforces this belief each time it says, "What do you think you're doing? You know that's not you. You don't do that. You've never done that."

Connie was a woman who was taught the value of her intellect. Being smart was prized in her household. "It was the only thing that was rewarded. Even being athletic didn't matter. My sisters and brother, and I had to be smart."

Her family disdained people who paid attention to their appearance. "Dad would say, 'A lot of nice clothing on their backs and nothing in their heads. Let's see how far that gets them.' I don't recall him ever acknowledging that any of us looked nice, even Mom."

Connie bumped into this piece of baggage – her family's LIES about you're either smart or you're attractive – as she attempted to move into a leadership role that required public interface on behalf of her employer. She was seen as smart, technically brilliant, but her appearance didn't match the professional image her company wanted its representatives to project. She was hard-pressed to understand the company's position.

"I'm better qualified than anyone for that job and everybody knows it. I'm not going to put on lipstick and high heels and strut around like I'm a stupid bimbo."

Wow! I think she was channeling her father. Blinded by her myopic way of thinking, she believed she could be smart or attractive, technically competent or a dim-witted bimbo. She was locked into either/or, exclusionary thinking. She didn't see she had the winning combination that both smart and attractive created.

She refused to flex. Locked in LIES, Connie listened to messages from *The Border Patrol*, messages that she used as the reason to not change, to not go to her *growing edge*. As a result, she remains imprisoned in her old role — all because she was led by the LIES of *The Border Patrol*. Cozy in her familiar comfort zone, she is still smart. But, she was not smart enough to realize *she* cheated herself out of an opportunity for expansion and growth. The request was reasonable — dress in a manner consistent with our standards and our customer's expectations for professionalism. Her *"that's not me"* response turned out to be self-limiting.

Do you use binary, exclusionary thinking? If so, what does it cost you? At times when you have opted to use inclusionary thinking, what did you gain? Which way of thinking — exclusionary or inclusionary — has the most positive, lasting impact for you and all concerned?

Talking with a friend one day, she said, "I don't want Frank to come home this weekend. I'm too busy. I want to get my yard done and spend the evening with my girlfriends. But, he says he wants to help me. I guess I'll call him and tell him not to come."

"Why," I asked. Help seemed like a fine idea to me. I envisioned his assistance making the evening with her girlfriends possible. With help, she could feel more rested and refreshed.

"He's going to want to talk first, then we'll have to make something to eat, then he'll think we can spend the evening together. That's the way it goes," she explained.

She seemed to be holding the thought, "Either we have to do it the way we've done it in the past, or not at all." I suggested an alternative point of view that held potential for interrupting her pattern of either/or thinking *if* she wanted to disrupt it.

I began with, "What if you accepted his help *and* told him what you want the day to look like, today? With full information he could decide if he wanted to spend the day helping you or not. You don't have to stay in the pattern you've set, unless you want to. You could see about arranging to have his help *and* the evening with your friends. Maybe you can have *both*."

Her face lit up. She called Frank and openly explained what she wanted to do and why. He happily agreed to the change and confessed that he was thinking about seeing an old friend who would be in town. Inclusive thinking – the both/and approach – can often result in everyone having much more of what they want.

Think about the ways you can apply both/and in your life. For example, you can be a manager who has high standards *and* be respectful and compassionate. The two are not mutually exclusive; we just act as if they are. You can be feminine and strong. You can be masculine and sensitive. You can be a person who likes to plan and you can be spontaneous. Both are at your disposal.

You can love *and* feel hurt by what happens in the relationship *and* survive to love again. You can leave a relationship because it's no longer right for you *and* see that there is nothing wrong with the other person – you're just finished with the relationship as it is. You can be vulnerable *and* not be weak or get used. You can be loving *and* strong. You can be independent *and* still need others. You can be a superwoman *and* still need rest and time to yourself to rejuvenate. You can be feminine *and* athletic, or masculine *and* not athletic.

Being whole means you have access to both sides of any continuum of thought, feeling, and behavior. It's a matter of pulling yourself up out of your rut to see the options and choosing to explore and experience uncharted territory. You'll encounter *The Border Patrol,* but don't worry; with inclusive thinking you'll have more of your total Self, more of the full power of you, to bring to bear in every interaction with it.

Consider the ways inclusive thinking can expand your options and open new pathways for you. As you try out new ways of thinking and behaving, think in inclusive terms. See the new routes to freedom and your deeper Self this tool stimulates.

Woody's Way

Remember Woody from the Chapter Six? He was told to "marry a teacher, don't become one." Well, after years of doing work that paid well but was not aligned with his passion, Woody found a way to make a change. In fact, he earns his living doing what he loved as a child and continues to love today. Director of Learning and Development for a large corporation, he says in amazement, "I get to teach and make a good living."

Though it wasn't easy, he says, "The transition has been worth it." The road back to his original love required hard choices and a willingness to take risks – to step out into the unknown on faith. He spent time thinking through and identifying all that he had learned; all the skills and knowledge he gained through various positions and life experiences. He turned that information into a skill-based resume and went hunting for the right fit. Though the way was not clear and the outcome not guaranteed, he was certain about his decision to find a way to teach – to do what he loved. Woody's approach is one you can use to consciously transform your life.

*Woody's Process of Intentional Reflection and Conscious Choice
Resulted in Transformational Change*

1. Write down what you know you no longer want. Get it out of your system. This is a cathartic purge and the last time you'll focus on it.
2. On a separate sheet, write down what you do want. What is your vision of the contribution you'd like to make? What do you want to do most? Focus on what, not how.
3. You'll need a large sheet of paper for the next step. Create three columns:

   a. Jobs I've Held and Experiences I've Had
   b. Tasks I Performed / Goals Accomplished
   c. Skills I Developed / Utilized / Refined

   Working across the page, list your experiences; next list the tasks performed and goals accomplished; identify the specific skills you developed and used and refined in the role. Use a broad definition of experiences. They may include paid positions; internships; volunteer work; summer jobs; special educational or professional development; or travel experiences; etc.

   Mine your life, identifying all experiences that enriched you and will position you for the situation you've targeted.

Journal Your Truth

Which myths are you clinging to?

Which traditions or customs do you find confining?

Which piece of baggage — LIES — do you most need to shed?

Which tools will you use to support your process?

*Of the five **Pivot Points** included in **intentional reflection** and **conscious choice**, for you:*
- *Which are current competencies?*
- *Which do you need to give more focused attention to in order to master?*
- *How will you hold yourself accountable for your own transformation?*

If truth is always true, how much truth exists in your life? What can you say, without a doubt is truth? What is the truth you know?

*As you **align your energy and intentions** — feelings and thoughts — where are you most likely to experience a mismatch? Is it most often that your thoughts don't align with your goal? Or, is it more likely that your feelings are out of sync with your goal?*

*What do you need to do to create inner harmony — **aligned energy and intentions**?*

How might you benefit from thinking more inclusively?

*In which relationship or situation will you begin to **think inclusively**?*

Chapter Thirteen

You Aren't Who You Think You Are

❧

Three Layers of Your Being

After *Pivot Points* play their part in your development – particularly those shaping events that turn you away from your Spirit, you are no longer your authentic Self. The person or personality you think of as you is not the full story. The whole of you is much more than your idea of "good and bad" parts. In fact, the best part of you is covered over by your belief that these parts exist alone and define you.

You have three aspects, three layers, to your being: a mask self, a lower self, and a higher self. I was introduced to this concept about the whole of who we are through my work with a Core Energetics Therapist, and later, through five years of study at the Institute for Core Energetics where I received certification as a Core Energetics Evolutionary Therapist. I was also a member of the faculty.

If you want to learn more about Core Energetics, I urge you to do so. You'll find the Institute for Core Energetics on the web at http://coreenergetics.org. The model – mask self, lower self, and higher self – is also taught through the International Pathwork Foundation. You'll find the foundation on the web at http://pathwork.org.

I'll speak about the model in a straightforward, simple fashion. While I intend to make it accessible and easy to understand, the model is much richer and more complex than presented here. Further, the hard and important work comes in using the model to understand your crafty, complex personality. To get the most from what this conceptualization provides, I recommend working with a skilled Core Energetics practitioner or a Pathwork Helper. You'll find names and addresses listed on the Core Energetics website.

The Mask Self. The model describes layers to your personality. The top, outer layer is the mask self, the part of you that conformed to conditioning. Your mask is the set of beliefs and behaviors you adopted in order to fit in, be socially appropriate, and avoid punishment. Your mask is your public persona, the aspect most familiar to you, and others. It's the dimension of your being that you identify with most closely and readily.

It's the picture and story you present to the world. When we talk about saving face, the mask is the aspect of identity we're speaking about. Your mask is your self-image. It's what you want to believe is true about you, and it's what you project out into the world for others to see.

Everyone has a mask – a socially acceptable self, a public face. It's an adaptive survival-oriented tool that operates consistently with the ways you believe are necessary to ensure your safety, social position, and survival.

Believing you are your mask, you put forth a story and images designed to convince others of your mask's authenticity. In fact, a great deal of hard work goes into making your mask credible. Whenever your behavior, or that of another, surprises you, you're likely witnessing actions that run contrary to the familiar mask.

You'll go through a lot to defend your mask. Not allowing your identity, your self-image, to be challenged, you'll tell LIES to hide the truth of your thoughts, feelings, and actions. You'll fake the way you feel to save embarrassment or discomfort. You'll cover the thoughts you're really thinking and present ones you suspect will be more socially acceptable. It's the idea best depicted in cartoons with the broken line of circles going up from the character's head to the balloon above his head that contains his honest thoughts. Why do we do this? It's done with the objective of protecting yourself. We will do just about anything to guard our pretend self, keeping our mask – our pretend identity – safe from disturbance.

Truly, we are confused when we think the shadow is the light and the cover is the real thing. Make no mistake, your mask is NOT the real you. Comprised largely of limiting LIES, it has served you in that it helped you survive challenges, hardships, assaults, and affronts. Still, it is not your Spirit; it is your image of yourself – a reflection of ideas you have about who you are. It is your learned response to the world around you. Shallow, false, and constraining, your mask inhibits your ability to know your core Self, to live in the depth of the truth of who you really are.

The Lower Self. From our earliest days in the womb, things happen and we feel threatened. Parents who fight and scream; a mother who doesn't look you in the eye and talk to you lovingly; a father who doesn't hold you securely or affirm your presence; people who treat you in disrespectful and abusive ways. Such things, some considered a normal part of family life and other things – horrible things – happen to babies. The terror of the moment, or the pain of the constant, unchanging condition, marks the psyche. Damaged emotions take root and are fed. Lacking light and love, fear-based feelings settle in, just below the surface, breaking through, now and again. As the fear takes hold, it freezes into a fixed mindset, motivating behavior that works against our own best interest and deepest desires.

You're up against a fear-based, frozen mindset – limiting LIES – whenever you say, "I know I should…but for some reason, I can't seem to bring myself to. I mean to but it doesn't work out." Or, "I keep making the same mistake over and over again, no matter how hard I try." Or, "I say I'm not going to…but before I know it, I'm…again." This is the insidious sabotaging action of the lower self at work.

Containing qualities considered shameful, destructive, and dishonorable, hidden beneath the mask of your perceived identity, the lower self is the aspect of thought and behavior that's charged with negative emotion. Most of us disown the feelings of our lower self with, "How could anyone do that?" "I would never…!" We want to distance ourselves from such ugly, disdainful behavior. "That may be them, but it's not me."

A lower self thought or feeling is the kind "nice people" want to hide, turn from, deny, tell no one about it. Your awareness of its presence disturbs and invalidates your image of yourself as good and caring. Many of the thoughts and feelings, images and fantasies that live within the lower self are humiliating, disgraceful, terrifying, and hideous. People who do the unspeakable – commit murder, rape, mayhem – are manifesting the hidden content of the lower self. More challenging to acknowledge are the aspects of the lower self that also encompass more "normal" and socially acceptable ideas and emotions such as anger, isolation, withholding, intent to do harm, cheating, deceiving, victimization, hatred, rage, bullying – thoughts and feelings that are at the foundation of everyday acts of violence we witness and even participate in.

Everyone has a lower self, including you and me. Most of us work hard to keep the lower self under wraps, masked, out of awareness, out of view. We want to lose consciousness of its presence and we want to be sure it never spoils the view others have of us. The motivation to hide, cover over, the lower self is immense. We're relieved to bury it. The lower self is content allowing you to pretend it doesn't exist.

Sadly, when you make this choice – the decision to ignore your own negativity and destructive tendencies – unwittingly, you give free reign to the part of your mind and personality that distorts and destroys everything you value. Like a computer virus, it operates silently and invisibly in the background, until it unleashes its violent, ruinous fury, wreaking havoc in your life and the lives of those you touch.

The saboteur, critic, judge, naysayer, your lower self is not your friend. This aspect of your personality works against you. Defensive and oppositional, it will say and do things that ruin relationships or cause you to behave in a way that calls your integrity and credibility into question; or set up circumstances in which you make a poor decision that costs you your livelihood, family, or life's savings.

Maybe your lower self is like mine. Sabotaging my peace by pushing me to work way past the point of productivity, I call this part of me the Gestapo or slave driver. Exhausted and still moving, doing something, pretending to be productive, the automaton takes over. Guided by a distorted belief, better known as limiting LIES, I convince myself I have to be busy and productive at all costs, no matter how I feel. My lower self has no respect for my real needs and wants. It doesn't care about my feelings, peace of mind, or need to rest my mind and body.

Really, my lower self doesn't care about me at all. It would destroy me as quickly as it would destroy anything or anyone else. That's why it's so important to unearth it, acknowledge its presence, get to know it, and work on healing it. A Core Energetics Evolutionary Therapist, along with many other kinds of therapists and healing modalities, can be very helpful in this regard. Clearing away negative, destructive emotions is essential to wholeness and well-being.

The Higher Self. The lower self covers with the intent of smothering and suppressing your higher self. Your Spirit is your divine nature – perfect, limitless, pure, and loving. This is the miracle the mask and lower self wish to deny and hide.

Your core essence is love, kindness, respect, compassion, peace, and joy. The home of pure positive energy at your core, the center of your being, is your Spirit, your true Self – the real, unchanging you. You are a unique, individuated, embodied expression of God. Your core contains all of your spiritual talents, gifts, passion, positive purpose, and potential. Your work, and mine, is to uncover this truth. In order for us to be happy and fulfilled, we have to be – know, feel, and live – aligned with the energy of our core. We have to be the Spirit that we are and fulfill the Purpose we were born to manifest.

The Link to LIES. The mask self and lower self are the land of limiting LIES, the territory of *The Border Patrol*. The picture below tells the story. The mask self and lower self surround the real you, holding you hostage, keeping you imprisoned under a false identity, until you begin to understand who you really are.

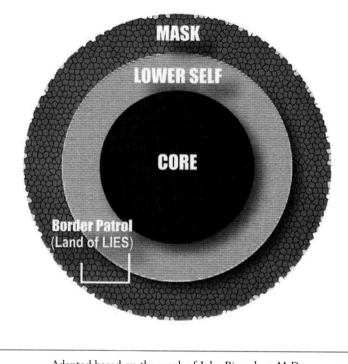

Adapted based on the work of John Pierrakos, M.D.

Founder, The Institute for Core Energetics

Author of *Core Energetics: Developing the Capacity to Love and Heal*

At your core you are Spirit having an experience in a body, as a human being, for a time. While you're here in this experiment, you have much to learn and contribute. Your biggest challenge and lesson is finding and following the route that brings you back to your core essence, your Spirit, the centerpiece of which is love.

Self-love, the Foundation for All Love

Self-love is the hardest love to acknowledge and give, and it's the most important. It's the beginning point, the foundation on which all else rests. Loving your Self means you are compassionate, non-critical, and nonjudgmental. It means going within to listen to your Spirit and find your truth.

Most of us are fairly competent at self-protection, self-defense, self-sabotage, self-criticism, and self-denial. Fewer of us know how to love Self. We prefer developing a mask we're comfortable with – one that projects the right image – and yes, the toxic material of our lower self.

Fear of the higher self is way too common. We deny the existence of our true Self and avoid opportunities to become familiar with our spiritual nature. Ignoring the call of your soul, you relinquish access to the lasting satisfaction of longing. Your real Self calls to you for acknowledgement, connection, and a place at the center of your life.

So many people ask for acknowledgement and love from others, yet they don't acknowledge, love, and honor themselves. They don't give to themselves what they want to receive from others. It's as if, with their hands behind their back, they open their mouths and say, "Feed me. Love me. Give me more."

When you connect with your core, and the simple tools and techniques throughout this book help you do that, you come to understand that love is who you are, naturally. You stop needing others to give you love, attention, approval, appreciation, gratitude, and acceptance. You give these gifts to yourself. This is how you feed and nurture yourself. In this way, you become a different person – one who is love, loving, and lovable.

Jim knows this story well. He longed for relationships in which he didn't feel ridiculed or put down. "I just want people who aren't out to use me. I want them to respect and appreciate me," he said. And, why not? You and I want the same thing from the people in our lives.

Raised by harsh, critical parents, Jim's sense of self-worth was underdeveloped. Never feeling he warranted the respect he was forced to give, his privacy and personal space were regularly violated, at home and in the outside world. Rageful about the way he was treated, but feeling powerless to change his circumstances, Jim's lower self was buried deep down in the catacombs of his mind. As he described the way he was raised, he sounded rational and objective, as if he had a handle on his history and had recovered from the pain of his past. But, he hadn't.

The pain of his past was evident in the present circumstances of his life. He was the humiliated boy – despite his forty-plus years – who still needed love and acceptance, but couldn't successfully organize the circumstances of his life to get it. The people who showed up demanded from him and gave little to him. The why of it all is complex, and he hadn't unlearned his early-in-life lesson: deny yourself and your own needs; give me what I demand.

Jim had no sense of his right to love, respect, and kindness. He wanted it but didn't believe it was his to have. Until he cracked that internal block, it wasn't likely he would find what he was seeking. He wouldn't be an energetic match to his desire. His healing must include learning to love, respect, and appreciate himself. He must become less self-critical and self-deprecating.

You've probably encountered people who are self-deprecating or self-critical. From time to time, I ask them why. "I've noticed you're quick to criticize your presentation and meeting facilitation skills. Why is that?"

The response usually contains some version of, "I do it so I don't have to hear negative feedback from others. If I say it first, they can't say that I didn't know I didn't do a good job." That twisted logic – I'll beat myself up before you have a chance to beat me – sets up a lifetime of agonizing mental pain. This is the recipe for long-term self-defeat and self-sabotage.

There are so many examples of the ways we disconnect from our Spirit and our gifts. When we do, we lose contact with our unique gifts – the special talents and abilities and preferences with which we were born and were meant to share with the world around us. When these skills are proudly utilized, you embark on a path that leads to greater effectiveness and contentment. You'll never feel you've settled, compromised, or given up the best of who you are in exchange for something less.

The King Serves the Queen

Everything that happens in your life establishes an opportunity for illumination; the opposite of illusion. There are no accidents. Each experience has something to teach us, when examined in the proper light, whether it is joyful or painful, seemingly insignificant or clearly important and impactful, long-lasting or short-lived.

At a deep level whatever you're teaching and learning is always for and about you. Insights gained can help you dispel the dark shadows cast by *The Border Patrol* and see through LIES. They help you uncover truth. Such was the case for me, with Ellie.

Up early one Saturday morning, I moved quietly as I got dressed, not wanting to disturb Bill. Easing out of the bedroom, I went downstairs for my morning ritual – meditation, a glass of water, a mug of coffee. Preparing for my day, I sat in the sunroom, thinking about what I would write. I was working on this book.

Trusting the process I now know so well – feel it first, believe it will come, then let it manifest – I was certain ideas would come into my awareness. It was simply a matter of time before I would feel the flow. I relaxed and kept my awareness open for the moment of clarity; ready to receive the answer whenever and however it would come. And, come it did, surprisingly through Ellie.

Funny, I hadn't thought of her in many, many years. But, thirty years later, there she was, the woman who had been Administrative Assistant to my boss.

She always seemed happy and excited about life. She glowed. Her eyes sparkled with unshakable confidence and self-satisfaction. Ellie exuded a life-affirming, energetic vitality; her joy was soul-deep.

I admired her despite our age difference. She had children my age and yet I enjoyed her company. Chatting about life, work, and relationships, we talked with ease and even saw each other socially, on occasion. I hadn't seen or thought of her in years, until that Saturday morning.

Her image and energy were with me. Ellie had come to remind me of an idea she introduced me to nearly thirty years earlier. Back then I understood it in a particular way. But now I saw another dimension of its truth – perhaps a dimension unfamiliar even to Ellie.

Married to Ray for more years than I had been alive, she and he still adored one another. To my surprise, these two people, the same age as my parents, were still sexually attracted to each other, the sparks between them hot and evident.

One evening, as Ellie and I talked over dinner, I asked her about her relationship with Ray, how they kept the fire burning after so many years.

Before responding, she paused, appraising my readiness for her message. Deciding she would trust me with prized information, she said, "A woman should choose a man who loves and adores her. He has to feel that way about her in order to acknowledge her as the queen she is to serve. In the light of his loving service, she'll be happy. In witnessing her happiness, he will feel successful and powerful...all because she's happy. Feeling like the queen she is, she'll treat him like the king he is. Loving his reflection in her eyes, the king will happily serve the queen."

My twenty-something-year-old jaw dropped. Ellie had my full attention. She continued. "Men have a hard time opening their hearts to love. They like imagining themselves as hard and tough. Love is soft and tender. They feel vulnerable in the presence of love – whether it's their own loving feelings or love being showered on them. Yet, love is the only thing that will make either of you feel safe and happy."

Having had experience with men who were afraid of their own tender feelings, I understood that. Even more important, I was aware of my own reticence about giving in to love. At that point in my life, I was fearful of feeling out of control and being vulnerable to the pain of almost certain rejection and loss.

Ellie continued teaching, encouraging me to choose well. "Be wise. Choose a man who loves and adores you. He needs to believe that you're special...more special, wiser, and kinder than he. When a man feels he has the prize of an amazing woman – a woman who helps him be a bigger, better man, he'll serve you well."

Slowly, she explained that when the man loves and adores her, the queen is able to lead with love and softness, keeping the love relationship and family strong and healthy. Loving his woman the man will feel good. He'll find no one and no other situation more attractive. Peaceful and loving, the couple's relationship will be safe and their sexual energy will remain vibrant.

She ended the lesson with, "He'll want to do all he can to keep what he has. In the end, the king will serve the queen."

Ellie didn't believe in settling for a man just because he says he adores you. No, not one bit. She believed that the adoration had to be real and flow both ways. If it didn't, you could find yourself unequally yoked. Each loving and cherishing the other creates a power balance important to every healthy and enduring relationship. When equanimity is lacking, an imbalance establishes the potential for disrespect and being taken for granted. Power imbalances lay the groundwork for emotional and physical abuse and even violence.

One of the LIES we live, when it comes to our mate, is "nobody's perfect." Usually, the speaker is saying, "I've been looking for a long time. While I don't really want..., she/he is all I've got. So, I'll make the best of it." This is settling for the lesser of two evils — the one you know, over the one you don't know.

Women tend to settle more frequently and readily than men, saying, "Yes" to a relationship because *a* relationship is better than *no* relationship. In the process, you sell yourself and the other person short. You may have a body in your bed, but the depth of connection and intimacy you both deserve is missing. Neither feels truly loved and fulfilled.

Now, back to the LIES we speak. "Nobody's perfect" is one of them. Perfection, as we mean it when spoken in this way, is an illusion. It's a fantasy of monstrous proportion, one of the Grand Design LIES that keeps you striving for an ideal, a false standard that neither you nor the other person can ever live up to, at least not for long — not beyond the period of romantic illusion. While the blush is still on the relationship, the other might look, sound, smell, and feel like your dream come true, but the appearance of "perfect" or "ideal" is usually superficial. It's just the person's mask. Peel back a layer and you'll find a normal human being, divine and perfect in his or her own right.

Usually when we talk "perfect" and "ideal," it's the child-mind speaking, asking for someone who meets all of our needs and wants and wishes — a fantasy person. Our focus is on getting the other to be and give us exactly what we want, when we want it, in the way we want it. It's a fairly selfish, child-like demand. The deeper truth is, people are perfect. We are all perfect just as we are. Not by some fake standard about how we *should* look, sound, or behave. Everyone is perfect and is at just the right spot on their path of evolution, even if you, or they, can't see it.

When we meet, we may recognize our particular brand of perfection is not right for each other. That's good to know. We can keep moving. Or, you may think you're right for her, but she doesn't feel the fit. When that's true, it's good to know. Don't get involved; you'll serve yourself and the other best. Keep moving. Don't settle. *Emotional equality* – the value of loving one another well, each feeding off and returning the good feelings generated by the connection – is too important to deny.

He's the Follower, NOT the Leader. Ellie's conversation was about individual people – women and men – in a heterosexual relationship. Later, I envisioned a deeper lesson in her message. What if she was talking about energy – masculine energy and feminine energy?

What if Ellie was directing my attention to the principle of masculine and feminine energy, both of which belonged to women and men equally? Was she showing me how the masculine aspect within each of us needs to serve the feminine aspect? How the masculine was not to lead, but to follow the lead of the feminine? That would be amazing!

Honestly, looking back, I balked at her comments that day. I couldn't see the sense, let alone the wisdom, she was conveying through all that talk about serving. It was the early 1980s and I was working hard to be a liberated woman. Of course that meant I was trying to convince myself, and everyone else, that I was just as good, as smart, as valuable, and as important as any man. I didn't realize my mindset and behavior were colluding with the precise problem Ellie discussed with me – the dethroning of the feminine.

Our culture, of course that means you and me, had come to value the masculine over and above the feminine. The vivid and visceral symbol of our dysfunction was the way our modern society made men the standard against which women were measured. Masculine, and more precisely male, values and behavior patterns were dominant, the accepted norm, prized as right. In this paradigm, the feminine, and more specifically women, pleased and served men. All things thought to be feminine were devalued and dishonored. To call a person, male or female, a girl or a sissy was the ultimate put-down. Disdain for all things associated with the feminine was pervasive and ranged from the diminishment and marginalization of women to absolute misogyny.

Women did not have equal access to opportunities in the workplace. Equal pay for equal work did not exist. Parity in education and athletic programs was not a reality. Women's voices in the political and religious arenas were marginalized or silenced. Even at home women took a backseat to men. The power of the feminine, embodied by women, was stifled, made invisible, forced into the background.

At that point in my life, I didn't comprehend the unintended consequences of the Women's Liberation Movement. Questing after the ability to be equal to men, I didn't understand that the movement further affirmed a world for women and men wherein feminine functions were devalued and disowned. I didn't see how women were unconsciously conspiring with men and perpetuating the illusion that masculine functions were more desirable, significant, and powerful than the ways of the feminine. I didn't see how the thinking that spawned and spurred the movement asked women to be more like men in order to get ahead.

The king, the masculine principle, became central. The queen, the feminine principle, was dethroned. The king ruled alone, without the benefit of her wisdom, compassion, and insight. He ruled from his head, not his heart. Logic prevailed. Emotions, feelings, and intuition were further devalued, pushed aside as soft, touchy-feely. These powerful qualities of intelligence became shameful, an invalid way of knowing. LIES about the indisputable accuracy of logical analysis, numbers, "hard" science, "provable" fact, and objectivity became our currency.

Masculine processes became the only real and valid ways of knowing. It's what we were taught to respect, trust, and use to guide our lives and inform our decisions. Feminine attributes and ways of knowing virtually disappeared from mainstream society.

Men <u>and</u> women denied the beauty, power, validity, and necessity of the wisdom of the feminine. As a result, LIES — all designed to lead us away from the wisdom of the feminine, away from our hearts and core into our rational, linear, mechanical minds — persist. Few of us, women and men, listen to or trust the guidance offered by the wisdom and voice of the feminine, the voice of Spirit.

Today, I know the head — the masculine principle — is intended to serve the heart — the feminine principle — not ignore it. After all, in the development of the human body, the heart is older than the brain; it develops first in the fetus. Wiser and more mature than the head, the heart — the throne of the queen — is the home of deep feelings, intuition, and universal knowing. It's *the* power center being the seat of love and compassion. Domain of the king, the mind is the seat of linear logic, reason, and analysis.

The masculine mind thinks in competitive terms — who will win and who will lose. Connected to all, the feminine heart opts for healthy, enduring solutions — wise actions that take into account the good of the whole. She loves and serves all. Alone, he serves himself.

In our present world, the wise counselor, the one who is connected to all and knows all, is seldom consulted. The one whose solution to any problem would be healing, not hurtful and divisive, isn't consulted. Her voice, even when she insistently whispers and tugs at consciousness, too often goes unheard submerged beneath conscious awareness. During those rare times when her voice penetrates consciousness, her words and direction are feared, not trusted.

Different from prevailing logic, her wisdom is unconventional. The solutions she surfaces and brings to awareness come from a deeper well far out beyond the land controlled by *The Border Patrol*. They come from the depth and wisdom of Spirit, holistic thinking, and intuition. Revering the masculine to the exclusion of the feminine is one of the LIES that led you away from your core, the truth of who you really are.

The Perfect Couple. You are a Spirit of Purpose. As such, you have access to the value and power of both the masculine and feminine principles within you. In fact, you are NOT whole without honoring and using both. The masculine part of you serves the feminine, and she loves him for doing so. She, in her wisdom, inspires and directs his actions. She is the constructive consciousness that he must obey if he is to be productive, happy, and satisfied. Together, they are the perfect couple, in a lasting, loving, passionate marriage.

Spirit of Purpose — feminine and masculine within — work together, loving and honoring one another. Spirit is the feminine energy. Purpose is the masculine energy. Spirit is inspiration. Purpose is intention. Spirit is wisdom. Purpose is focused attention and action.

Our work — yours and mine — is to be the Spirit of Purpose that we are. To accomplish that end, we must find a way to honor our masculine and feminine energy — our thoughts and feelings. We have to value equally the physical, seemingly fixed, tangible, material reality and the invisible, fluid, intangible, sensate, affective reality so that our inspiration and intention are in sync, creating inner harmony. When the masculine and feminine within each of us are in balance, internal peace will be our reality. When peace prevails within each of us, we will co-create and experience more peace in the world.

When there is internal alignment between the masculine and feminine, you are at full power. You have all the tools needed to be creative and fulfilled. Whole and complete, you are more inclined to work in favor of your Self — your Spirit. The masculine executes orders from the feminine. Her voice heard, the feminine fuels the masculine with tremendous creative ideas and sound solutions to problems. Seeing the brilliance and success she enables, he values her contribution and continually seeks her counsel.

The mental (masculine) and emotional (feminine) energies are effective partners. Emotional equals, each complements and completes the other. In their presence, conflict, uncertainty, disempowerment, fear, unworthiness, lack, a sense that something is missing, all diminish and fade away. Illumination occurs. The illusion is no more. The partners, Spirit and Purpose are together again and you have access to your full Self. You have uncovered the truth of who you really are.

You'll Always Want to Be Your Self

You will always want to be who you were born to be. That desire will never go away; it can't. It can only be covered over.

The more buried your awareness of yourself as a spiritual entity, the less fulfilled you feel. The less fulfilled you feel, the more you look for someone or something to blame or complain about. Before you know it, you're trapped in an unhappy vicious cycle, an unquestioned closed loop. Use the ideas and tools in this book to break free from whatever has you in bondage.

I know with certainty, you and I have a chance to look forward and forge the life we want. To do so, we must consciously choose it and remain faithful to the choice to be our real Selves.

Journal Your Truth

Describe your mask — your public persona.

When you interact with others, what image do you try to convey?

How does your mask serve you? How does it limit your satisfaction and success?

What characteristics of your lower self — your negative thoughts and feelings — are you aware of?

What impact does your lower self have on your life?

Which aspects of your logic are distorted and result in patterns of self-sabotage?

Identify and list your higher self qualities.

In what ways do you fear or resist your higher self?

Which of your higher self qualities do you:
- *Express easily and consistently?*
- *Want to allow into fuller expression? Which LIES must you release in order to do so?*

Which is the leader in your life — the masculine or the feminine?

With which — feminine or masculine — are you most familiar and comfortable?

What are you longing to express and experience? How can valuing and utilizing the feminine and masculine equally support you in having your desire?

Chapter Fourteen

Uncover the Truth of Who You Really Are

❧

The Tussle and the Tango

The journey to reconnection with your Spirit and Purpose requires you to stay strong in the face of predictable challenges.

After a period of steady progress, Joe — the handsome achiever who found relationships with women eluded him — had a setback that surprised him. "I know what the issue is now, and still it's no easier; no guarantees. I started to feel the new relationship getting close — we were developing real intimacy — and the same old stuff came up. I got scared and wanted to run. I thought I'd be through with this by now. It just never seems to go away."

The vast majority of people who attempt fundamental change have experiences similar to Joe's. The mental *Border Patrol* will arrest you, hold you hostage, and pressure you to step back into familiar territory. The pull back to the old familiar rut will be strong and seductive.

It's as if *The Border Patrol* says, "Careful. Don't go any further. You're not safe here. We know the old place. Let's go back there. It's comfortable. We know what to expect. Why do you want to change things, anyway? This is just the way you are. You can't change. See, I told you it would be too hard."

The temptation to half-step or back-step intensifies at points along the journey. You'll tussle with the force of habit as it beckons you back to well-worn grooves. You may feel the magnetic pull in time to grab hold and stand your ground before the slippery slide begins. All too often though before you know it, you'll find yourself reunited with your old pattern, wondering what happened. Questioning how you ended up back here, in precisely the place you swore you would never return.

Skillfully and consistently, you'll tussle and tango with *The Border Patrol*, keeper of the status quo. Stay strong and committed. Break through the boundaries of the LIES you live. This is just the kind of intersection where *conscious choice* can lead to *transformational change*.

Courageously confront your internal *Border Patrol*. Reexamine your use of the word *can't*, and other phrases you casually speak every day, accepting their meaning as fact. Can't, the negative of can, signifies un*able*. Fact is, in most instances it isn't that you lack the ability to do something, in truth, you are un*willing*. Unwilling is not the same as can't.

Can't defines ability. Unwilling is more akin to won't. Won't is linked to motivation, not ability. In most instances a lack of change or progress is reflective of your level of motivation and willingness, rather than your ability. So, if nothing else, you can at least be honest with yourself about what you really mean. If you are honest with yourself, you'll notice a marked change in your sense of clarity and integrity – and you'll feel and be trustworthy in other areas, too.

Perhaps you know someone who says, "*I can't lose weight*," or "*I can't stay for the party*," or "*I can't play the piano*," or "*I can't get ahead*." In actuality, the person could lose weight if they ate less and exercised more; stay for the party if the party was a priority; or learn to play the piano with the right equipment, instruction, practice, and perseverance; get ahead if they were willing to figure out what it takes to get ahead in their company, and do it.

Tussles and skirmishes with *The Border Patrol* will be stimulated and enabled by the unconscious ways you limit yourself through language and your willingness to quickly surrender to its authority. Instead of fighting with *The Border Patrol* – giving it your energy and attention – tango with it… dance. And this time, you lead. Take over, and craft the steps to be ones of your choosing and liking.

Forget the tussle. Tango!

The Grand Work of Spirit

The work of Spirit is grand. Accordingly, everyone's spiritual purpose is grand. In my twenties, I began vigilant, fervent prayer to know my purpose. I was tired of waking up with the feeling of "Is this all there is?" And I was certain my life was about something more valuable and enduring than the experience I had created.

One day, visiting a church in North Carolina, I prayed my prayer throughout the service: "God, what is my mission? Why am I here? What is my purpose? Help me know." That July Saturday evening, the answer came. It sounded simple – like the Golden Rule, in a way. I heard and understood that my mission is to "love everybody."

But, when I "heard" the answer, quaking, I knew it wasn't simple. It was significant; I could feel the power and gravity of it. Overwhelmed with emotion, crying uncontrollably, I felt pure joy, bliss, and awe. My body felt lighter and a depth of happiness and a peace filled me. Up until that point, I had never known such a totally wonder-filled feeling. Finally, I knew what my life was about. I knew my purpose, my reason for being!

What I didn't know was how to apply those words to my day-to-day behavior and interactions. What does "love everybody" mean? How do I do it? Intellectually, it seemed obvious, given my Sunday school training. But, everything about me – my thoughts, feelings, and actions – fell short of that admonition. I prayed more.

Prayer sends us inward. It takes us into the quiet inner reaches of our being, the only place where we can connect with the Divine. Our quiet inner space is the home of the Divine, the sanctuary of Spirit. It doesn't always occur to us that we are the Divine being with whom we want and need to connect as an extension of God, we have available to us all of the resources of the Divine creative energy of the universe. We only need to go within to make contact with everything we are, and with everything we need.

Finding My Spirit of Purpose

Going within, I found a quality of stillness I didn't know existed. At times, my mind would stop its incessant chattering. Screeching messages of fear, worry, and anxiety, which were commonplace in my internal conversation, subsided. A rare gift in those days, a sense of gentleness and peace would fill me. Soon, clarity began to dawn on me concerning what "love everybody" meant. To this day, its full meaning continues to be revealed.

Living life and unfolding as a Spirit of Purpose is a perpetual process. "Love everybody" involves loving each person; honoring all people equally; supporting others in finding and living in alignment with the best of who they are. And, I came to understand that "love *everybody*" included me. That was the hard part.

Loving others was a part of what I had been taught by Mom, Granny, Sunday school teachers, and the pastor. One of the Ten Commandments – "Love Thy Neighbor as Thy Self," (Mark 12:31, KJV) – these words were prevalent in the culture even though in practice it was rare. The bigger more perplexing matter was what it meant for me to love me. I had a sense of what loving others might involve. I had no notion how to even begin loving myself. The idea was not yet in mass consciousness or cultural conversations.

Think about it. Do you give thought to loving your Self? *Really?* If so, who or what do you love? Your "good" qualities – the ones you were socialized to show? Your "bad" qualities – the ones you were socialized to hide from others, even from yourself? Are they the dimensions of your Self you are to love? Yippee to sharing the good side of your public face! Yikes and Yuck to bringing the shadow side to light! But, the good news is, that's not all of you. Some might say, that's not you, at all.

Born with a Purpose

"Is this all there is to life? Why am I here? What am I to do? For much of my life, these three questions ran through my head, continually. Many of my clients confess to entertaining similar questions. You have to ask questions to destabilize your static definition of yourself and get to the truth of who you really are.

The more I asked my three questions and noticed what occurred to me, the more insights I received. Time and again, I would read or hear something that agreed with my belief that I was born with a Purpose and for a specific reason. Affirmation that I have something in particular to contribute to the world around me, as does everyone, showed up regularly through books, articles, and conversations. While I had no idea what my Purpose was, certainly I wanted to know; I prayed to know. And, I received my answer.

Now, every day, to the best of my ability, moment by moment, I live it. I know I'm a spiritual being having an experience in human form. Though I appear imperfect, the beauty of my reality is that I'm right on the mark, moving toward the learning I need to continue unfolding and realizing the fullness and wonder of who and what I am.

Spiritually, I'm perfect, as are you. As a human being I do things that make the reality of my wholeness imperceptible. I face situations, make choices, and do things that suggest I have forgotten my power, perfection, and Purpose. Seeing me, you might judge me as less than the grand and magnificent being I am. I make the same mistake with you. We're blinded to the deeper, miraculous reality of our true Self and that of others.

My friend and colleague Kyle told me a story about her and her best friend from college. She said, "We used to call each other 'perfect' as a way of acknowledging that we were flawed, dealing with our disappointment in relationships and wanting others – particularly guys – to see us as good enough. But, deep down, we also believed that in our imperfection we were perfect...just as we were created to be." Though motivated by a search for relief from the pain of rejection and disillusionment, these young women spoke deep truth. They pushed themselves in the only way they knew how, at that point in their lives, to challenge their beliefs, look within, and know the reality of who they were. They made an earnest attempt to not allow their sense of value to be defined by what others said or how other treated them. Intuitively, they knew feeling good about who they were was a choice – a choice they had the power to make.

It's All About *You*

You don't have to challenge anyone else's beliefs or behavior, just your own. Be responsible for your Self. Change your thoughts and behaviors.

Focus on yourself. Question your thoughts, feelings, and actions. Take care of your needs. Devote your energy and attention to improving yourself by connecting with your core. Make no one else your special project – "You Just Do You." Energize and follow your dreams and watch a transformation occur. Your knowledge and acceptance of your Self will deepen, and so will your love for the real you.

What I'm suggesting doesn't give you license tell others off, cut them down like a tall poppy, or act in ways that are rude, insensitive, immature, or irresponsible. In fact, I'm encouraging the opposite. Be self-responsible and accountable for what *you* think, feel, say, and do. Be responsible for the choices *you* make and the consequences *your* decisions create. Blame no one, not even yourself, when outcomes don't live up to your expectations. Less-than-desired results provide an opportunity to analyze the situation, connect with your real desires, and make a new choice that will move you closer to the end you seek.

Throughout the process of "You Just Do You," accept the fact that you are not able to control anyone else. The pressure you apply, or guilt you attempt to induce, is not respectful of others and their preferences. Just as you do, they have a right to be exactly as they are. They have the right to pursue their goals and dreams, just like you. And, they have a right to make choices with which you don't agree. Too often we want others to behave in particular ways so that we feel more comfortable.

Our job is to teach ourselves how to remain centered and content, irrespective of what others are doing, or not doing, to or for us. Learn to be comfortable following the path you construct, even in the face of an unfavorable reaction from those around you. While you may not carry the intention of making choices that cause others to feel unhappy, there will likely be times when that's the case. Stand firm, courageously committed to your decision. You don't have to defend your choice or convince anyone of its merits. You just have to Just Do You and live with your consequences.

Talk of consequences may feel to some like a threat. But, let's be clear, there are always consequences. There are consequences for decisions you make and actions you take. And, there are consequences for indecision and inaction. You don't think of the pain you endure in unhappy situations as consequences. You're so familiar with the situation it just feels like life. But really, you're facing the effects, the consequences, of previous decisions – decisions you haven't changed or made anew. A byproduct of the conscious and unconscious choices we make, consequences can't be avoided.

When it comes to "You Just Do You," you can do it. On any given day, at any moment, and in any situation, you can choose in favor of your Spirit and Purpose, or you can work against your Self. One choice strengthens you. The other weakens you. One choice calls forth your core Self, the other your limited, little self. Choose wisely, in service to your success and satisfaction.

Reclaim Your Passion and Purpose

Most of us have areas in which our growth and self-expression were cut off – areas where the best of who we are was denied or actively discouraged. Something obvious, or subtle, or beneath our conscious awareness, covered over our genius, opposed our passion, and drove us off course.

Some experienced the blessing of people who encouraged and reminded you of your gifts and unexplored capacities. These are the people – parents, teachers, family members, community members, colleagues, characters in books and movies – whose influence served as affirmative *Pivot Points*. These experiences helped to establish your solid foundation.

Somewhere within, large or small, there is a place where *Pivot Points* dashed your hopes, veiled your vision of excellence, shielded your memory to the truth of what you love, curtailed the exploitation of your natural abilities, and doused the remembrance of your deepest dreams. This place represents your *growing edge* – the place where you left the aspect of your Self that you now need in order to feel whole. Reconnect and reclaim your lost parts – the parts that remain perfect and hold the awakened energy of your Spirit, passion, and Purpose.

It's All About YOU! YOU JUST DO YOU, and No One Else!

If you catch yourself thinking or saying to another:
- "If only *you* would…, I could…"
- "*He* won't…, so I can't…"

- "I want to…, but it won't work *because she*…"
- "I wish I could…, but *they* won't let me…"
- "I can't get *them* to agree to…, so I can't…"
- "*They* won't listen. I can't get *them* to…"

STOP!
You're about to limit your options based on what someone else will or won't do.
You're blaming others for the condition your life is in — conditions you've created.

Journal Your Truth

Why are you here? What is your Purpose? How can you uncover it?

What do you feel called to do with the gift of your life?

In what ways is The Border Patrol holding you hostage?

What is your growing edge — the place where you left aspects of your Self you need in order to feel whole?

How can you, more and more consistently, choose in favor of your Spirit and Purpose?

Chapter Fifteen

It's Your Life

CXD

Favor Your Desires

It's your life. Listen to your heart and soul, look around and gather data about what you like and want. Remember what has always called to you; what you love doing; what makes you feel most alive and joyful.

Decide and take action in favor of your desires — what you think and feel is right for you. Pay close attention to what occurs as a result. The consequences you experience — those that align with your desire and those that don't — all create opportunities to learn and become even clearer about your intentions and what works best for you.

Many people resist deciding and acting for fear they'll make a mistake. Don't worry; most often you'll feel as if you have limited information and no guarantees. Get used to it. There is only deciding based on what you know now. Acting based on what you've decided. Learning from what happens as a result of your decision and action. Then, take the next steps you feel guided to take to move you closer to your dream. That's it.

LIES tangle up your thinking, causing you to believe it's more complicated than that. It really isn't. You can believe LIES. Or, you can employ the power and simplicity of your unchanging truth.

Love and Use Your Gifts and Talents

Be true to the real you. Love your gifts and talents. Use them as a demonstration of self-honor and self-appreciation. Whatever your gifts are they're given so you're well equipped to carry out your Purpose. There's a need for you and what you have to share. Your gifts serve you <u>and</u> they serve the world. No matter how different from the norm, no matter how usual, unusual, or just plain weird, you and your gifts have a place that is uniquely yours. The world is full of interesting, unusual, diverse opportunities. Don't miss out on the ones that call to you by becoming someone or something you're not.

Recently, I learned about a man who has an atypical passion; one I've never heard of before. His name is Mike Rutzen. He was interviewed by Anderson Cooper of CBS's *60 Minutes*, on a segment called "Great Whites: Diving With the Sharkman." Mike lives in South Africa and swims with and studies great white sharks. That's right, I said great white sharks. Yes, they're the ones we think of as man-eating predators. But, not Mike; he sees them differently.

According to Mike, these creatures aren't aggressive and deadly. They're simply curious and interested beings, with social personalities. In a quote from the episode, Mike says, "There's no universities to teach you what these animals' social dynamics are and social behavior is. And the only way to find that out is by getting into the water" with them.

Anderson Cooper tells us that "Rutzen is not a scientist. He was born on a farm and knew nothing about sharks until 20 years ago, when he began working as a fisherman along the rugged coast near Cape Town. These waters are home to the world's highest concentration of great whites." There, he began his groundbreaking relationship with the great whites and is educating the rest of us about these heretofore unstudied fish.

Mike Rutzen is not stymied by convention, but instead, is guided by his passion and sense of Purpose. He marches to the beat of his own drummer. Do you?

Take note...passion and Purpose, inspired by Spirit, always does good. It expands your capacity to love and be a positive, compassionate force in the world. Its power may be expressed through the work you do or simply through your very being – your presence and impact – or both.

Painting a New Picture

Judy followed the path of *should* until she was in her early forties. That was the point where she felt she just couldn't take it any longer. With great care, she led herself through a process of *intentional reflection*. She learned how to make *conscious choices* – choices guided by inspired ideas of what she wanted to be and express.

Judy did some mindful planning, left her work as a mid-level manager in the insurance industry, and went to art school where she received a BFA. It's what she always really wanted. She said, "I just decided to listen to my Self for a change."

And change she did. Her life has only gotten better and better. She is a joyful artist, finally living in alignment with her Spirit and Purpose.

That's Why I'm Here

I met Sheila during one of our St. John visits. She was a shuttle driver at our hotel. One evening, Sheila drove Bill and me the three-minute ride from the beach, up a rather steep slope, to our room.

"Good evening," she said as we boarded. Her voice sounded happy. "Good evening," I replied. I said, "You sound joyful," acknowledging what I heard in her tone and saw in her body language.

Without hesitation, she said, "Oh, yes; I am. I wake up every day feeling happy to be alive. And you know what?"

I didn't and admitted so. "No. What's that?"

"I've always been like this. I want to be happy every day so that I can help someone else have a good day. It gives me a good feeling when I am positive. It's contagious."

The shuttle grumbled and groaned all the way up the hill, but not Sheila. When we reached our stop, I slid off the seat and told her, "You've made my day. I'll always remember you."

"That's what I like," she said. Turning to me, she smiled and said, "That's why I'm here: to help people feel good…to spread a little positive cheer. That makes me feel good, too." Smiling brightly, she disengaged the brake pedal and drove off shouting, "Have a good night. Hope to see you again."

Agreed: I hoped to see her again, too. I will always remember her because Sheila knows her passion and Purpose, and she lives it every day.

If you think, "She's 'just' a shuttle driver," think again. There's no "just" when it comes to living your Purpose. When you wake up in the morning, looking forward to your day, you've won the hardest battle you'll ever fight — you are living true to your calling. Living your Purpose makes you happy!

Journal Your Truth

Which of your desires would you like to favor fully?

What steps can you take to do so?

Which of your gifts and talents could you use more frequently and to greater effect?

Is there a new picture of you and your life you would like to paint?
- *Describe it in detail.*
- *Notice your thoughts about your new picture.*
- *Be aware of how you feel about it.*
- *What must you do to align your energy and intentions so that you are positioned to expect, receive, and enjoy the experience of your new reality?*

Chapter Sixteen

You Are a Spirit of Purpose

૯|૭

"Be the Change You Want to See"

Uncovering the truth of who you really are, you will feel better and your life will improve. It's not that all of the challenges go away, they don't. But, you'll have greater comfort and competence to deal with them. You'll not allow yourself to be knocked off base, be taken off course, or lose connection with your Spirit and Purpose.

Many people, in fact everyone with whom I've ever spoken, want the world to be a better place. That idea and ideal may mean something different to each of us. Pointing to different aspects of society and social institutions as the targets for change — whether it's less violence in our homes and communities; greater equity and respect in the workplace; healthier partnerships within families, communities, organizations, and politics; an improved educational system; more accessible, adequate health care for all people; reverence for the environment and mother earth; effective relationships with all global citizens; world peace; or fairness, justice, transparency, and integrity — we have to realize and acknowledge that change in the world happens most effectively when we change our hearts and minds. Change on that level — change within — leads to lasting social shifts.

Revolutions can create upheaval in the social order through swift, frequently violent, and decided disruption. Legislation can mandate movement from one set of laws to another, theoretically forcing people to behave differently. History tells us our response to new laws is slow and, until we become committed to the new requirement — or are severely punished enough for noncompliance — real change eludes us. We may make noises or take actions to present the face of compliance, all the while continuing to do what we've always done.

Because our thoughts and feelings guide our actions, change will occur most successfully when we, person by person, transform our hearts and minds — when we shift the way we think and feel. The world will change when we change. As we change and become more of what we want the world to be — more honest, just, transparent, respectful, peaceful — we'll see that difference manifest in the world around us, more and more. We are influential. Our way of being — our energy and intentions — are impactful. As we improve the tone of our small slice of reality, we have an affect on everything and everyone around us. In every task we perform, in every interaction we have, the power to create positive *Pivot Points* is ours.

Mahatma Gandhi said, "*Be* the change you want to see in the world." ***LIES That Limit: Uncover the Truth of Who You Really Are*** lays the foundation for the personal transformation Gandhi's statement suggests, and his example sets. When you discover the hidden, negative impact limiting LIES have on your ability to be the powerful, positive, purposeful Spirit you are, you will have laid the groundwork for your own transformation.

You are a *Spirit of Purpose — one who practices Intentional Reflection and makes Conscious Choices that lead to Transformational Change in yourself and the world around you. As a Spirit of Purpose, you are committed to constant growth in your ability to live from the center and deepest, purest part of your being — your Spirit — and you lead your life aligned with your calling — your Purpose.*

When you rid yourself of the crippling constraints of limiting LIES about who you really are, you'll be given the gift of inspiration from your higher Self. With that will come greater freedom to be who you were born to be. Constructive engagement with your world — your inner and outer world — will be stimulated by the wise muse or teacher that lives within you. Your presence, the way that you show up in the world, will be influential and make a real difference, one that benefits you and adds value to everyone your life touches.

Author's Biography

❦

Teressa Moore Griffin is an international consultant and executive coach, specializing in self-awareness and executive development. Founder and CEO of Spirit of Purpose, LLC, her work focuses on developing leaders who are self-aware and committed to using their power — personal and organizational — to serve the interest of *all* stakeholders.

Having held key positions in major corporations, Teressa's professional experience spans the pharmaceutical, financial, retail, and consumer products industries. Her diverse client list has included the American Express Company; AT&T; AstraZeneca; Barnett Banks; Consolidated Edison; Forest Laboratories; GlaxoSmithKline; Harley Davidson; Merrill Lynch; The Prudential; Texaco; The United Negro College Fund; and The Thurgood Marshall College Fund.

Since 1977, she has been a consultant to executives, managed organization-wide strategic culture change initiatives, and designed and implemented numerous leadership development processes and programs.

At the heart of Teressa's work is a belief that self-awareness and the ability to forge effective partnerships with stakeholders establish the foundation for sustained success. Her experience, undergirded by interpersonal competence, professionalism, and compassion, enables her to support others as they confront complex business challenges and evolve as leaders.

A professional speaker, as well as a former adjunct faculty member at The American University/NTL Institute's Masters of Science in Organization Development, Teressa has been published in the areas of workforce diversity and effective intercultural communication. She is a qualified user of the Myers-Briggs Type Indicator and the DiSC Personal Profile System. Additionally, she is a certified Organization Workshop trainer, a Power Lab coach, and a Core Energetics therapist.

Educated in Psychology, Organization Development, and Human Resources Education, Teressa is a graduate of Beaver College and Boston University. Her memberships have included the National Training Laboratories Institute (NTL); the Organization Development Network; The Women's Leadership Collaboration; and The Forum of Executive Women.

With a lifelong commitment to supporting the growth and development of people, Teressa is especially skillful at helping others achieve their desired results. She has the gift of clear sight, coupled with an ability to effectively deliver feedback, support internalization of the data, design actionable development plans, and encourage personal accountability.